Michael Baughen

THE MOSES PRINCIPLE

LEADERSHIP
AND THE
VENTURE OF FAITH

HAROLD SHAW PUBLISHERS
Wheaton, Illinois

MOSES AND THE VENTURE OF FAITH
Copyright © 1978 by A. R. Mowbray & Co. Ltd.
ISBN 0 264 66524 4

Published in the United States of America as
THE MOSES PRINCIPLE: Leadership and the Venture of Faith
by special arrangement with
A. R. Mowbray, England
First Printing, 1979

Library of Congress Cataloging in Publication Data

Baughen, Michael A
  The Moses principle.

  1. Moses.   2. Bible.   O.T.Biography.   3. Chris-
tian life1960-   I. Title.
BS580.M6B29   1978   253   78-27498
ISBN 0-87788-558-3

Printed in the United States of America

CONTENTS

FOREWORD
by David Winter

There can be few churches nowadays that have never experienced the urgent need for a large sum of money. Dry-rot in the floor, leaks in the roof, purchase of a parking lot or tottering of a tower can suddenly present a hard-pressed congregation with a financial crisis. Equally, the desperate need for a youth center, or more Sunday School rooms, or a public address system can face church members with a similar dilemma.

The traditional answer is an "appeal," which usually means putting one of those "thermometers" outside the church, or organizing car washes or walk-a-thons and generally subordinating the energies and enthusiasms of the congregation to the over-riding task of pushing up the sum raised towards the target indicated. Sometimes—often—the money is raised, but at an enormous cost in energy and time and frequently a corresponding loss of spiritual commitment. As a sad by-product, the church also sometimes earns a local reputation for being materialistic.

In this book, Michael Baughen suggests an entirely different approach—what he calls the "venture of faith." It demands nothing in terms of fund-raising, but everything in terms of faith. Instead of car washes there will be prayer; instead of thermometers outside there will be fervent Bible studies inside the church.

If this seems a somewhat impractical approach to the intensely practical business of raising large sums of money, let it be said that not once, but twice, when Michael Baughen has put this theory to the most stringent test it has worked. The money has been raised, every penny of it, without any public appeal, without gimmicks, stunts or fund-raising activities. And not only has the money been raised, but the spiritual temperature of the church has been raised, too.

It may also seem rather odd to suggest that the first step for a congregation towards raising, say, $50,000.00 for a new roof is to study the life of Moses. Yet that *is* what Michael Baughen is proposing and this book is specifically designed to help them do it. He believes that the answer to a need in the physical realm is to be found in the spiritual realm, and that faith is the divinely appointed key that unlocks that answer. He discovered this principle while studying the life of Moses, and has twice shared that experience with his congregations, with remarkable results. Now he has put it on paper, in his own easy, conversational style. Who knows how many churches may find their whole financial situation revolutionized by studying it?

David Winter

INTRODUCTION

In the summer of 1964 we moved to Manchester as a family to take up the Rectorship of Holy Trinity, Platt Fields, Rusholme —known affectionately to most people simply as "Platt." The church was the only surviving example of such a building made of terra cotta, and, as I was instituted, a diocesan official heartened me by saying "I pity any man who takes on a terra cotta church." The rectory was designed on the grand scale— for a rector with a very large family, and servants. It had potential, but it stood formidable and gloomy, dark varnished wood almost everywhere, its stained glass windows soaking up the light of even a summer's day. When we had gone to look at the place the previous rector's wife had entertained us in the lounge wearing a coat and scarf—necessary before heating was installed. The congregation was a faithful nucleus numbering around a hundred, but with warm hearts and with their spiritual feet on the ground. They gave us a great welcome, with a marquee on the lawn for the induction and many expressions of love and support. Yet the task we all faced together was daunting.

The church building stands on the edge of a park, but at that time it served a fairly typical city area with a corner store at the end of most streets, numerous bars and the Manchester City football ground right alongside. (Weddings have to be arranged so as not to clash with matches when the City team is playing at home, and the prayer meeting is carefully scheduled for a different night from the midweek home game!) The old church hall, some way from the church, was in a terrible state —all right for the hard bashing it received from some of the activities that went on in it, but certainly no "home" for a church family to meet in. The old Victorian rectory's size was an asset in coping with a lot of the church's programs.

My wife and I knew that God had called us to Platt. He had marvellously sealed it as his plan for us. My experience over the previous years of travelling round the country on deputation had given us a country-wide outlook. The Lord put everything together for us. The one date that was possible to go and see the church and parish was the one day that Myrtle was able to travel at that point of carrying our youngest child. She had been unwell right up to the day, and then again after that day for a different reason. I was already scheduled to be in the area and the Platt Church Council was also booked to meet that evening, having changed the date several times before fixing it. There was an immediate sense of unity with the committed group of believers who were the core of the church. All signals were "green" and this was a great help to us in facing the task ahead.

That task would have been overwhelming without the Lord, but the possibilities *with* the Lord in command were limitless, both in the parish and in the University close at hand. It was in fact through the student scene that the Lord particularly helped us, but through Oxford, not Manchester University. The OICCU (Oxford Inter-Collegiate Christian Union) held a pre-terminal conference each year and they had asked me to be with them that autumn, before their October term began, to give two addresses on Moses. I had accepted a long time before and now began to regret it! Not only did it mean travelling away from Platt for a few days, but it was demanding of me a thorough study of Moses that would take days to prepare —days I could ill afford at that time. I debated whether to ask them to let me change the topic but, mercifully, decided against doing so and gave the Bible messages as requested. It was to be a turning point in my ministry for, whatever it did for the students, it main effect was upon myself.

The burning question that repeated itself over and over again as I prepared was: Did I believe in *that* God? The God who brought his people out of Egypt and who pulled back the waters of the Red Sea, was he *my* God—the God whom I worshipped through Jesus Christ now? Did I really believe in God *as God?* (It's a question I have put to many others since, regarding the object of their faith). Was God able to do great things for us in the situation at Platt? Indeed, the more I thought about it the more it became clear, that above all else the characteristic of Moses' life and leadership was not that he had *great faith* in God, but that he had faith in a *great God*. Faith can be (and often is) as small as a grain of mustard seed but if it is faith in a great God it can bring tremendous results in the work of His Kingdom. God invites us to believe in him in this way, in such glorious passages as Malachi 3 or Isaiah 40, or in a record such as that of Hebrews 11, with uncomplicated faith demonstrated in exploits and deliverances and even in what the world would call disasters. It is this dimension of faith in a great God that can open up the most formidable situations, for our God is the God of the Impossible.

Moses' leadership experience was impregnated with this faith and from it spiritual leaders (and all of us) can learn lessons that are relevant in our Christian lives. Indeed, what I would call the "Moses Principle" has transformed me, and the two churches I have worked in, since I first discovered it that autumn. Walk in the steps of Moses now! Make the Moses Principle your foundation for living faith!

PART I
MOSES–MAN OF FAITH

I
THE
EARLY
SHAPING

What an amazing upbringing Moses had! Like Wesley, many centuries later, who saw himself as a brand snatched from the burning, Moses was a baby snatched from the bulrushes, destined to become one of the great national leaders of history, even to be portrayed by Burt Lancaster on film thousands of years later!

Yet this child's upbringing was in itself amazing. On one hand he was privileged to receive the finest education offered by the world of his day—being a part of the Pharaoh's own household; on the other hand he was to be personally cared for by a truly godly woman—his own mother. It is one of the delightful ironies of the story that when Pharaoh's daughter advertised her need for a nurse, it was Moses' own mother who was hired for the job! Dick Lucas, Rector of St. Helen's, Bishopgate, once told a group of candidates that entering the ministry was like being Moses' mother—you do the thing nearest to your heart and get paid for it!

The double influence of a nurse-mother with a heart for God and the secular education of one of the highest households of the then civilized world provided a unique foundation for this man who was chosen to be the leader of God's people. You can see him emerging into manhood, impeccably courteous (note how he stands and helps the daughters of the priest of Midian in Exodus 2:17), perhaps a little pampered and yet with that enormous potential within him like a coiled spring ready to burst into action and change the world. But he had a lot to learn—and there were three major factors in the next stage of his shaping by Jehovah.

A Sense of Sin
First, he had to be made keenly aware of the reality of sin:

> One day, when Moses had grown up, he went out to his people and looked on their burdens; and he saw an Egyptian beating a Hebrew, one of his people. He looked this way and that, and seeing no one he killed the Egyptian and hid him in the sand. When he went out the next day, behold, two Hebrews were struggling together; and he said to the man that did the wrong, 'Why do you strike your fellow?' He answered, 'Who made you a prince and a judge over us? Do you mean to kill me as you killed the Egyptian?' Then Moses was afraid, and thought, 'Surely the thing is known.' When Pharaoh heard of it, he sought to kill Moses. (Exodus 2:11-15)

Over-confidence
Many a modern young man or woman will find themselves in Moses' position, particularly if they have had a fairly privileged upbringing—a comfortable home, a good education, perhaps a college degree. The potential is all there, but not always the maturity to go with it. Maturity cannot be reached by short cuts. It comes through attending the school of life and it takes many years to reach graduation. Youth can be a time of dangerous over-confidence. I remember my own

bravado just after earning my driver's license. Disdaining my mother's pleas to drive more slowly along the driveway next to our house, I hit the gate-post!

Youth can be a time of throwing off restraint, with our formal education past; of feeling freedom from the influence of home, freedom to do just what we want to do and how we want to do it. As Christians we need to be aware of this danger-area, to remind ourselves frequently that we are still sinners and that we are still prone to sin, even if we are "in Christ."

Learning the Hard Way

Moses had to learn the lesson the hard way. As he went out to visit his own people he realized the weight of their burdens and burned with indignation, finally boiling over when he saw an Egyptian beating up a fellow-Hebrew. This was no time for protest marches, safely at arm's length (and usually much further!) from the action. The problem was right there in front of him and with the casual glance from left to right that we might associate with a person feeding his parking meter and making sure that the policeman is not looking, he killed the Egyptian and buried him deep in the sand. It seemed to Moses a neat and simple solution, and in its way, quite satisfying—until the next day. The realization then that he had been found out, that even his own people did not approve his action and that he might well have been wrong in what he did, hit him like a hammer blow. The further fear that Pharaoh would find out about it sent him off in the opposite direction with all possible speed.

The consequences could have been much worse. Indeed, some people's whole lives have been darkened by having to live with the results of such impetuous action, uncontrolled passion or overconfident decision. If we think it couldn't happen to us, let us be warned. "There, but for the grace of God, go I" should be a phrase often on the Christian's lips. When we see great men such as King David arranging Uriah's death so that he could take Bathsheba, or Peter denying Christ, we need to pray for daily grace to recognize that we are never beyond the possibility of sin. Moses learned this with a great shock and it profoundly influenced his life.

Who is Shaping Us?

How far had Moses' action been merely a replay of what he had often seen done in Pharaoh's household? His thinking and acting must have been influenced by that environment in spite of his mother's private instruction and example. Paul's words in Romans 12, "Don't let the world squeeze you into its mold," should be written up on our bedroom or bathroom mirrors, a daily reminder of the way in which the attitudes of others, the standards of society and the mass media, the books and films of our times are inevitably, imperceptibly nudging at our minds and shifting our values.

If you happen to be short-sighted like me you may remember that you only gradually noticed that the outlines of the world around you were growing indistinct. You tried to fool yourself all the while that you could see as well as ever. Eventually, when you went to the optometrist and looked through the lenses he placed in front of your eyes, you understood, with amazement, how much you had been missing. The change in your vision had been slow, gradual. The lenses simply showed how far the deterioration had gone! The influence of sin is just like that. Awareness is the key here; prevention is better than cure and if you find you *have* been changed by the world in which you live, thank God for his mercy in putting his lenses in front of your eyes and suddenly showing you just how blind you have been. David's experience of deep heart-searching and repentance as expressed in Psalm 51 may become vividly relevant to you at such a time.

The crucified "I"

C. S. Lewis expressed it cogently when he described his self-examination "with a seriously practical purpose," on coming to Christ. He says that he "found what appalled me: a zoo of lusts, a bedlam of ambitions, a nursery of fears, a harem of fondled hatreds. My name was Legion."

Professor C. E. M. Joad, renowned for his part in the B. B. C. "Brains Trust" series at the end of World War II, was a forceful atheist until the latter years of his life. His conversion to Christ was precipitated over this issue of sin. He admitted that all his Utopian hopes for a new society had been doomed to failure because they did not take into account the fact of original sin.

Any man who is to be mighty for God must get this clear. He must see himself as he really is and as he stays close to the Cross of Christ he will see himself increasingly clearly, not in morbid introspection but rather in the light of the reality of sin and the necessity for the daily refilling of the Holy Spirit, so that the crucified "I" is balanced by the indwelling Christ. John Newton could testify, at the end of his life, "There are two things I *can* remember: I am a great sinner and Jesus Christ is a great Saviour!"

Solitude to Stop and Think
Second, Moses needed solitude in order to think through his situation.

> Now Moses was keeping the flock of his father-in-law, Jethro, the priest of Midian; and he led his flock to the west side of the wilderness, and came to Horeb, the mountain of God. (Exodus 3:1)

Slow Down!
"The backside of the desert" is how the King James Version describes where Moses went. The RSV calls it "the west side of the wilderness," perhaps a more geographically correct designation. But whether we want to call this the "West Side Story"

or the "Backside Story," it was a place of solitude. Moses was truly alone there. This is not a condition with which most of us are familiar. For most of us, life consists of bursts of activity with gaps for leisure—work pressure and pleasure pressure. Most 20th century Christians are "activists" rather than "contemplatives," rushing from one meeting to another, praying here, discussing there, fellowshipping somewhere else, speaking, arranging, befriending, supporting, evangelizing and always at work. How easily all this activity can become a substitute for "the real thing" so that if our activity is removed our whole Christian existence collapses too. Imperceptibly it has shifted its foundations from Christ to the work-schedule; and however exciting and enjoyable our activity has been, as a life-foundation it proves to be sand, not rock.

We all need to learn the lesson of solitude, of quiet listening and learning from God so that we can maintain firm foundations even in the midst of much activity. The Christian should not be lazy. But while he should be "at work in the fields of the Lord" it should never be at the expense of his spiritual roots.

Blessing in the Silence

For Moses, the solitude in the wilderness was not a matter of choice, but it still was turned, by God, into a time of blessing! If God places us in the desert, or allows us to be there, it may be one of the most important times of our lives. All the props have been removed. Our cherished dreams have faded and gone. The superstructure of our lives has crumbled into dust. We may be ill or alone. Matthew Henry has a good word for us in such a situation: "Let those that think themselves buried alive be content to shine like lamps in their sepulchres—and wait till God's time comes for setting them on a candlestick."

The Discipline of Time

Yet solitude and quiet alone with God *can* be a matter of choice, a deliberate part of our plan. Moses frequently went away to be alone with the Lord in the following years. Some people laugh at the idea of discipline, regarding it as somehow unspontaneous, even unspiritual. Jesus did not laugh at it. Even the Son of God needed to be alone, to spend time in his Father's presence. Paul didn't laugh at it. He "buffeted his body," prayed constantly, and even used his enforced imprisonments profitably. Discipline is not a matter of law, but of love—a longing to learn, to be corrected by God, to live more fully for him, to hunger and thirst for his Word and to live out his righteousness. How we need to discipline our time!

Restoring Perspective
Solitude has another great asset. As the dust of activity settles we begin to see things in truer perspective. We more easily discern what is more (and what is less) important. We can see the way ahead more clearly. We can glimpse significant landmarks on our path so that later, when we are immersed in activity again, we can still navigate with certainty.

Not only in our personal lives but in national and world events we need to see with God's eyes, to view with his perspective. As storms build and disappear across the world and Christians in many places undergo bitter persecution, even annihilation, we see how easily it could happen to us too, as followers of Christ. The storm may break with rapidity and violence. Before it, and during it, we need to have learned the secret of solitude. Remember, in Psalm 46, the concept that it is God who is our refuge and strength in spite of earthquakes, wars, even worldwide destruction. The key to that confidence is found at the end of the psalm: "Be still and know that I am God. I will be exalted among the nations. I will be exalted in the earth."

Or take the situation in Psalm 73. The writer feels overwhelmed by the success of the corrupt and wicked of the world and the problems of the believers. He finds his true perspective restored only when, in verse 17, he goes into

God's sanctuary. Then he sees everything differently and the psalm concludes on a magnificent note of faith and triumph. Let us learn the habit of being quiet in God's presence so that day by day we do not focus on the problems, with God seen somewhere in the blurred background, but start the day seeing God at the center, shedding his light and his help on the problems, showing us his own perspective.

Sensitivity to the Lord
Third, Moses learned to be sensitively aware of God's presence and power.

> Suddenly the Angel of Jehovah appeared to him as a flame of fire in a bush. When Moses saw that the bush was on fire and that it didn't burn up, he went over to investigate. (Exodus 3:2-3 TLB)

When the Bush Burns
The burning bush must have been a remarkable sight in that lonely place. It was certainly more noticeable because it was not seen in the confusion of other events. When Moses realized that the bush was afire but not consumed he turned aside to observe this extra-ordinary phenomenon. *Then* God spoke.

This kind of sensitivity that "God is in this" grows in us as we experience more of the way in which the Lord is at work. The super-spiritual person who constantly prefaces his remarks with "the Lord told me" is often only attaching the Lord's name and authority to his own wishes or ideas. If we really believe that something is "of the Lord" we will say so with humility, recognizing that we could have mistaken the signals. This is where the confirmation of others in the body of Christ has its marvelously correcting and confirming effect. When, after discussion and prayer we can say together, "It seems good to the Holy Spirit *and to us*" we are most likely to be on target. Sometimes, when God's call or conviction burns upon our hearts in solitude with the Lord, it is wise to share it with a close friend for confirmation. When I awoke to God's call to the ministry, the positive response in me was immediate (it was during the reading of announcements during a service!) but the reinforcement of this conviction took place over six or seven months as a group of close friends made it a matter of special prayer.

Out of the Rut

However, being humble and careful about God's word to us does not mean that we need not listen for or expect his direct communication to our hearts. There are some Christians who wouldn't notice two hundred burning bushes all flaming away at once! They gave up expecting God to guide or challenge them ages ago. They are like the inhabitants of the Australian outback where, it is said, the muddy roads dry into deep ruts and a notice is put up: "Choose your rut carefully. You'll be in it for the next thirty miles!" They have settled into their rut—buying a house, mapping out their career to retirement, raising their family, counting on a comfortable life, involved at the appropriate social and church levels. Of course, they have heard that the Bible speaks about being "strangers and pilgrims" but they'd never expect God to change the course of their lives now—after all, they're in their forties!

I am reminded of a man comfortably settled into suburban London life with a good job. He was a lay reader in the church and even preached from time to time. One Sunday, after a sermon, an elderly lady came up to him and said "Mr. Jones, have you ever thought that God might want you in the ministry?" He thought it very funny—until later the same day another elderly lady, without any collusion save that of the Holy Spirit, said to him "Mr. Jones, have you ever thought that God might want you in the ministry?" This time he didn't laugh. Instead, he kneeled down and said "Lord, you don't want me in the ministry, do you?" The Lord did. The man obeyed, went through college even though he had a growing family and is now in the ministry.

But you see, it was the first time for a long while that he had said to the Lord "Am I where you want me to be?" The two old ladies were rather unlikely burning bushes, but he saw and turned aside—*and God spoke.* So keep open to the Lord every day (and don't despise the counsel of elderly people—they're often the praying backbone of a church). Ask God daily, "Am I where you want me to be? Am I doing *what* you want me to do, *how* you want me to do it?" Stay sensitive to the Spirit. Expect God to be involved in your life. Listen for his voice; wait for his touch; then you will know when "it is the Lord."

Discussion Questions

1. Consider all the ways in which you and your church use time. Is this use of time disciplined? Is it re-evaluated from year to year? Is it effective?

2. On what basis should we (individually, or as a church) decide what is important for us to accomplish?

3. What tests would we apply to a proposal or strategy to discover whether "God is in it"?

2
KNOWING GOD

Waking Up
The sight of the burning bush awakened Moses to hear the voice of the living God. Sometimes it takes us a long time to reach this point.

It's so easy to hear the gospel, to witness to the faith but not until later to realize the shallowness of our Christian knowledge and experience. It is then that we begin to want to know God; not just to know *about* him but to know *him* deeply and with utter honesty and reality. This can be the real breakthrough in Christian experience. The Bible begins to light up with fresh significance and impact. We hunger and thirst for more of the Word. We begin to experience God speaking *to us* as we read it. Yet it may have taken years of superficial Christian involvement before we wake up to the close and startling voice of God calling to us.

He Knows Us by Name
When the Lord saw that he turned aside to see, God called to him out of the bush, "Moses, Moses." (Exodus 3:4)

The first revelation to Moses is that God knows him! Here is the God of the Universe, creator of the whole earth, addressing this speck of humanity *by name*. Mystery and mysticism are the keynotes in the religious thinking of many, today and throughout history. But the Bible is the book in which God says, time and again, "Behold, I show you a mystery." God is the revealer of hidden things, the door opener, the letter-in of light. The Bible shows us the living God as the one who reveals himself to us personally.

God not only introduces himself to us—he knows us through and through. Jesus saw Peter both as what he was and what he could be. Nathaniel was amazed that Christ could describe his character so quickly and so accurately and asked "How do you know me?" Jesus knew and understood such diverse individuals as the rich young ruler, the woman at the well, Levi the tax man, Nicodemus, Judas. And he knew whom he was calling as disciples. In John 10, the picture of the Lord as shepherd includes the fact that "He calls his own sheep by name."

No Veneer

To anyone who is called to follow and serve the Lord, this is both a startling and comforting truth. It teaches us not to fool around with God; not to pretend; not to hide (or think we can hide) any side of our character from him; not to think that the slick spirituality which may mislead our friends is impressive to God. Such a deceptive veneer is sickening. A good antidote is to turn to the Psalms and observe the frankness with which the psalmist speaks to God, even to the point of bluntness. Let us never try to impress God or our fellow humans by making ourselves out to be anything but what we really are. The deepest Christian friendships I experience are wonderfully open. In the framework of the love of Christ I can reveal myself honestly without fear of rejection and can turn my own clear scrutiny on the lives of my brothers and sisters in the

Lord without injuring or demeaning them. Christian truth thrives in such an atmosphere of honest love.

Comfort

Yet the same truth is greatly comforting. It is natural to feel that we cannot cope with leadership in God's service. Jeremiah's cry, "I do not know how to speak; I am only a youth" is echoed by us all. At the same time we are thrown back on the wisdom and strength of the Lord who is calling us. He knows our weaknesses and gifts better than we do ourselves. He knows our internal conflicts, our uncertainties, our insight, our intelligence (or lack of it). He also promises to equip those he calls. I find this enormously comforting as I often shudder at the weight of responsibility in the service of God. Who am I, fragile and inadequate, to be engaged in such work? The rock-certain answer is, "Because God has called" and he knows all about me. Knowing God, then, begins by realizing that he knows us—totally, completely.

Our God Is Holy

And Moses said "Here am I." Then God said "Do not come near. Put off your shoes from your feet, for the place on which you are standing is holy ground." (Exodus 3:4-5)

Moses' awareness needed further broadening. He had to learn about the holiness of God. His casual answer, "Here I am" was quickly followed by the removal of his shoes—and a sense of profound fear.

It is surprisingly easy to treat God casually. We arrive at a church service late because we think our time is more important than his (though we wouldn't ever phrase it quite like that). We approach worship without prior thought, reflection or preparation, just as if we were attending a football game or a movie. We dream our way through a service (just as we may do in our personal time alone with God), dwelling on everything but the Lord and his Word. We make promises to God in times of spiritual crisis and easily forget them when our lives have fallen back into their "normal" patterns.

In God's service the reality of his holiness breaks in on us slowly. Whether we are leaders in a church organization, or officers in our student group, or Sunday School teachers— only gradually do we wake up to the fact that this is *God's work,* that we are working and speaking in *his name* and that we are functioning as parts of *his body.*

This realization burns hard into the preacher's or teacher's heart. When I was first ordained I was quite sincere about preaching but did not give it the major preparation it required. The longer I have been serving God, the more time I have needed to prepare for preaching as I have come to feel, increasingly, the enormous responsibility of handling the Word of God and of teaching and expounding it to others. The paradox of preaching is that it is both a joy and privilege as well as a burden and serious responsibility. Jesus uttered these heart-stopping words as he commissioned the seventy to go out in his name: "He who hears you hears me. He who rejects you rejects me." (Luke 10:16)

In God's service we bear the divine coat of arms and the words "By appointment to the Lord." The boldness which is ours because of Christ as we enter the holiest is matched by the exhortation "Let us offer to God acceptable worship, with reverence and awe."

Our God is holy.

God's Greatness

God said "I am the God of your father, the God of Abraham, the God of Isaac and the God of Jacob." (Exodus 3:6)

The greatness of God now began to overwhelm Moses. "I am the God of your father . . . of Abraham, Isaac, Jacob. . . ." This was no minor, territorially confined God but the God of the history of the world. Open your eyes, Moses! Realize how God's purposes have been working out through the generations until now. He is the sovereign God.

This truth is just as alive for us today, thousands of years later. History is stretched out behind us like a great, intricate carpet. And over and under and around it all is God. We can trace the pattern by which God's purposes have been worked out in spite of all the attacks of the enemy.

Those who are called to serve the Lord (that is, all of us) need to hold firmly to this truth of God's greatness, for we will be called upon to trust beyond human reason, to defy logic, to launch out into the deep and dare for God, to face the impossible without flinching or falling back. And that is what the school of God is all about—to prepare us ahead of time, with smaller trials, lesser risks, for the tests of the future.

Involved in God's Work
The Lord now emphasized that what Moses was being called to do was *within the divine plan and purpose*. Moses was not being asked to start a work in his own strength. It was not his ideas and abilities which would be tested. Instead he was being called by God and would be equipped by him. Moses was to be the channel, the servant, the tool, the agent, but not the director. The thrust of verses 7-10 is entirely in that direction: "I have seen ... I have heard their cry ... I know their sufferings ... I have come down ... I will bring them up ... I will send you." There is no doubt who is in control!

So the fundamental question asked by any servant of God, any church board or committee, any student in the school of God is, "Lord, what is your plan and purpose, and how can we put it into action?" That is the question. But we must be prepared to listen and obey when the answer comes and the way is made plain. It is easy to come up with all sorts of creative ideas to carry out a piece of work for God but it will be wasted effort if it is not in God's time and according to his purpose.

I hoped to start a men's group at Platt for years but never received confirmation that this was God's plan. Then a time came when a leader was available, a relatively new believer, but one who could bring freshness and vigor to the work among other men. God set his seal on the plan and gave it great fruitfulness. Proverbs 19:21 sums it up well: "Many are the plans in the mind of a man, but it is the purpose of the Lord that will be established."

God Is in Control

But Moses said to God "Who am I that I should go to Pharaoh . . .?" When one is in the Lord's work, an immensely comforting realization is this, that the ultimate responsibility is his. Moses' plaintive response "Who am I that I should go to Pharaoh and bring the sons of Israel out of Egypt?" sounds somewhat feeble after the Lord's strong revelation of his purposes, but it's natural! And perhaps it is a healthier reaction than the thought, "I can easily cope with this job." One preacher, responding to an invitation to come and preach in a new area, replied "Pray that I might be nothing." He received his answer: "You *are* nothing, but we still want you to come!"

A direct answer to Moses' question "Who am I?" might have devastated him. God's answer came, instead, in terms of a divine guarantee: "Certainly I will be with you." And that was really all that mattered. It is the guarantee always given by God at the moment of stepping out into new territory for him —to Isaac, Joseph, Joshua, Gideon, Saul, Isaiah, Jeremiah and to every follower of Jesus Christ in Matthew 28:19-20: "Go and make disciples of all nations . . . and lo, I am with you always, to the end of the age." It is a guarantee which bears, on the other side of the coin, the words, "Without me you can do nothing."

Take God from Moses and Moses is nothing. Take God from us and we are nothing. Yet *with* God, and *in* him, we are sealed by the I AM—the unchanging, all-powerful, actively self-revealing, gracious, covenant-keeping, eternal God.

Discussion Questions

1. How does the fact that God *knows* us (understands us through and through) affect our attitude to doing work for him?

2. What are the advantages, and what is the cost, of being "open" to God and to others?

3. What factors determine whether a Christian project succeeds or fails? How do these factors affect our approach to this project?

3
FROM PREPARATION TO PRACTICE

The Tension of Faith

Can anyone affirm that learning to walk by faith is easy? An honest and heart-warming description of the real tension that exists between the faith-path and the sight-path is given to us in the story of the journey made by Ezra, in Ezra 8:21-22. He proclaims a fast with a call to prayer and an expression of dependence on God for, he says, "I was ashamed to ask the king for a band of soldiers and horsemen to protect us against the enemy on the way; since we had told the king 'The hand of our God is for good upon all that seek him.'"

One part of Ezra wanted the army. The other part wanted to believe God, though trembling. The Lord's honor and reputation were involved, so Ezra stepped out in faith. How much blessing is missed by some Christians and some churches because they are wary of launching out with God and would rather calculate their resources, limiting action to the knowable and foreseeable. How can God be honored by confidence in human resources alone?

Excuses

Then Moses answered, "But behold, they will not believe me...." (Exodus 4:1)

God matched Moses' continuing excuses with his own provisions and answers. When Moses protested, "They will not believe me" the Lord provided an authenticating sign as he did again, centuries later, to validate the messiahship of Jesus and the apostleship of the twelve. "I am not eloquent" Moses complained. So God appointed Aaron, his brother, as his mouthpiece (though Moses did pretty well as a speaker once he got going!) God is in control, and when he calls he equips and prepares the ground ahead.

As Moses learned this, he found his faith being even more severely tested. Pharaoh's heart turned as hard as the bricks the Hebrews had to manufacture, and Moses cried out in despair, "Why did you ever send me?" (Exodus 5:22) God replied, "Now you will see what I will do . . . I am the Lord."

Caught in a dilemma that would make most people give up on the spot, Moses was about to see God's glory manifest. So impossible would the situation become that it would be crystal clear to everyone that deliverance from Egypt was by the power of God alone. The servant of God must trust the overall purposes of God which may be far more marvelous and far-reaching than he can anticipate.

Impossibilities

The Egyptians pursued them. (Exodus 14:9)

If the delivery from Egypt seemed to grow increasingly difficult the trap at the Red Sea appeared impossible from the start! With the waters stretching out in front of them, rocks and forts barring the side exits and the army of Egypt rapidly approaching from the rear there seemed absolutely no escape.

Yet it was God who had brought them there and Moses' schooling in faith was now gloriously proved in practice. He had no workable answer to give the fearful people. He could not say how the problem would be solved. But he believed in God as Deliverer.

It was Hudson Taylor who said that there are three stages in any work of God: "Impossible, difficult, done!" And it was Brother Andrew who observed that we should leave the possible efforts to unbelievers and encourage believers to tackle the impossible. George Muller is well known for his great work of building homes for orphan children but it is not so well known that he began that work in order to prove to himself and his fellow-believers that God responds to faith.

Whether we meet "Operation Impossible" in our personal Christian life or in our corporate activity as a church community, let us thank God that he is allowing this test in our lives! This is our chance to prove him as the God Who Is Able, the God of the Impossible.

Reaction

And the people of Israel cried out to the Lord, and they said to Moses, "Is it because there are no graves in Egypt that you have taken us away to die in the wilderness? What have you done to us in bringing us out of Egypt?" (Exodus 14:11)

Moses did not carry all the people with him in his stand of faith. He faced fear on their features and in their cries of protest that turned into personal attacks upon him as their leader. One of the prices of leadership is the probability of opposition and criticism. And often it is, as it was in the Red Sea dilemma, not so much a personal attack as an expression of individual frustration, fear or inadequacy. Because a Christian is a leader, he is the obvious target because he should be Christian enough not to answer back! If we are sensitive people, we may find this sort of criticism very hard to bear, even if we know the reason behind it. We may feel like giving up and at such a moment we are exposed to the attack of a far more deadly enemy.

Firmness without Fear

And Moses said to the people "Fear not, stand firm and see the salvation of the Lord, which he will work for you today; for the Egyptians whom you see today you shall never see again. The Lord will fight for you and you have only to be still." (Exodus 14:13)

Moses' reaction here was splendid. He had been in God's school and it really shows! First, he put his finger on the cause of the panic—fear. "Fear not" he shouted boldly. Only a man who is looking beyond the circumstances to the living God can say such words in such a situation. Centuries later, it was the same with Paul in the storm-buffeted boat on the Mediterranean Sea—all cargo thrown overboard, the ship disintegrating, the weather worsening and all hope of being saved completely gone. Paul came on deck and said "Take heart, men, for I believe it will be exactly as God has told me."

A Chinese friend used to give advice on how to worry best. Don't worry at night, he counselled, because you will lose sleep and get tired; don't worry at mealtimes or you will get indigestion; don't worry while working or it will affect the standard of your work. Instead, choose a good time to worry and at that appointed hour go and be alone, with your Bible open and your spirit listening to God. Then, he said, you will find that your worry has disappeared! That is the Red Sea situation translated into terms of practical Christian living—and the principle is the same: look at God, not at the circumstances.

Don't Panic!

"Stand firm" is the next command. There was nowhere to run anyway. But if we let fear swamp us we may spend a lot of time running around in small, useless circles. Yet the thrust of this command is the thrust of faith—God *must* help us and it *must* be now. There was no alternative.

But how? How could God deliver them? Without knowledge of the details, somehow they knew he would. Their part at that moment was to *be still*—a clear demonstration that their faith was in God. The Hebrew word used here has the idea of ploughing and suggests a deliberate and purposeful act of quelling fear and covering it over with peaceful trust; not waiting for the right emotion but consciously fostering a trustful attitude of mind. It is at this point that faith in God becomes a choice, a vote of confidence in one who can do what we cannot.

As Isaiah was to say, from the context of his own set of difficulties, "You will keep him in perfect peace whose *mind* is stayed on you." God invites us to throw our burdens on his infinitely capable shoulders, and that means letting them go, not holding on to them after we have prayed about them. His peace is possible at the heart of the most impossible crises.

Go Forward!

The Lord said to Moses, "Why do you cry to me? Tell the people of Israel to go forward. Lift up your rod, and stretch out your hand over the sea and divide it, that the people of Israel may go on dry ground through the sea." (Exodus 14:15)

Impressive though Moses' stand has been up to this point, he has a new lesson to learn about faith. Standing still in the midst of problems may be an expression of trust, but going forward *into* the impossible is a greater one. We need to be clear, however, that we do not walk into the impossible just because we choose to do so, and then expect God to deliver us. We should move ahead only when all other avenues are closed, as when Paul was forbidden by the Spirit to go in various directions and then found himself on the sea coast of Troas, to be called by God across the sea into Europe. When every door is closed and God clearly tells us to go forward, that is when the impossible becomes possible!

In the faith-project at All Souls we faced the fastest national rate of inflation in our lifetime, rocketing up at a speed of 25% a year, so that our estimated costs were multiplying geometrically. As this involved sums of hundreds of thousands of pounds, we had to ask ourselves "Dare we go ahead?" But God had so sealed his purpose in our hearts that though we could not see how we could possibly get through, we could do nothing but go forward. We could not deny the call and leading of God by retreating. In the Lord's amazing power and grace he brought us through free of debt, to his glory. We saw the *impossible* become the *difficult* and then the *done*.

God told Moses that through the great deliverance in his immediate future for them at the Red Sea "the Egyptians shall know that I am the Lord." In success achieved by man's effort, man gets the glory; in ventures of faith where God leads us into and through the impossible, *he* is glorified.

My God

> Then Moses and the people of Israel sang this song to the Lord . . . . (Exodus 15:1)

So the waters were parted and the people of Israel crossed over on dry land. The Egyptians were confounded and destroyed. The impossible had happened! For Moses and the people it was a time for praise. How quickly they all turned from complaining and fear to praise and thanksgiving! Their song of praise speaks of God as the God of history, but clearly rejoices in him in personal terms: "This is my God." Ventures of faith sort out our priorities. They show us our real selves. Secondhand faith, merely cerebral trust in God, an arms-length relationship with our Father is exposed when we have to trust the Lord in real and practical ways, whether in crossing the bed of the Red Sea, or in sacrificial giving during a building project, or in facing any one of a number of personal challenges in our lives. Our faith has to be first-hand, something to be acted upon as well as held in mind. So often difficulty forces people out of the shadows of Christian faith into its glorious sunlight. From the heart they can praise God for his greatness, a God majestic in holiness, for they have seen him act in power before their very eyes.

Covenant Love

You have led in your steadfast love the people whom you have redeemed. (Exodus 15:13)

The climax of this outburst of praise rises from the root of their relationship with the Lord. The Hebrew word *Hesed* is one of the most precious of the Old Testament. It is translated as "mercy" in the King James Version, as "steadfast love" in the RSV, but perhaps is most precisely expressed as "covenant love." It is the unchanging and committed love of the Lord for his people, sealed in covenants (or binding agreements) several times in the Old Testament and for us in the new covenant of Christ's blood spilled for us. It is covenant love on which the psalmist rests and to which he refers more than a hundred times. It is covenant love for which God pleads through Hosea (Hosea 6:6) in place of empty sacrifices. It is covenant love on which the prophets rest their faith in the heart-turmoil of exile. "Give thanks to the Lord for he is good and his steadfast love endures for ever."

The Party Is Over

They went three days in the wilderness and found no water ... and the people murmured. (Exodus 15:22)

The praising and rejoicing came to a rather abrupt end. Miriam packed her timbrel and the Israelites set off on the next stage of the journey. After their experience, you would think further doubt would be impossible! The progress of the people of God would surely be one of firm faith and delight from now on. But three days without water and they were grumbling again. How human, how true to life, even among the people of God. The large-scale ventures of faith are all too often followed by trouble in relatively insignificant things. Moses discovered this. So did Joshua and Nehemiah, and Paul!

God allowed his people an immediate solution to the water problem, but in fact he had already made an ample provision of twelve springs and seventy palm trees at Elim, just a short distance ahead. He knew they needed water. He had in mind a much better provision than the temporary sweetening of the waters of Marah. If only they had trusted him they would have arrived there sooner. Were they rebuked in heart at their lack of faith? It seems doubtful, for on the next stage of the journey they faced hunger and started grumbling again, this time for Egypt, with all its wonderful food!

Faith in Action

This kind of faith takes a lot of learning. At a houseparty in Austria we had spent our evenings studying the latter part of Isaiah, from chapter 40 on. What thrilled our hearts was not just the awesome effect of those passages but the setting in the majesty of the mountains. By day and by night the majesty of God was made real to us. On our last evening together the inward glow of faith in such a God was sobered by the remark "Will God now test us to see if we really believe in him as our great God?"

He did, and the test was in very practical terms. First there was the disappointment at the discovery that our final morning together, reserved for shopping, was wasted. All the stores were closed for a holy day. Then the hotel served our lunch so late that there was barely enough time for our bus to drive down the mountain road and make the train connection at Innsbruck. The bus roared away only to turn a corner and find a new road barrier announcing that the road was closed.

Those who were nervous about the tight schedule already were ready to give up, until the bus driver got out, shoved aside the barrier and sped on towards Innsbruck, where the train had already pulled in, packed with other tourists and with no reserved car for our party. More cries of frustration! At Calais one of the girls collapsed in the customs shed, the result of a toxic insect bite back in Austria. She had to be carried onto the boat. The Health Officer at Folkestone was radioed and asked to meet the boat. Then the party missed the train to London.

Myrtle and I missed all this adventure because we returned by car, but when the letters came a few days later it was clear who had learned lessons of faith and applied them. Some letters opened with the words, "You will have heard of our dreadful journey back from Austria." Others began, "You will have heard of the wonderful way the Lord provided for us on our journey back from Austria." The same journey, but viewed in radically different ways! While some had been panicked at Innsbruck Station, others had been cheerfully distributing German tracts. When some had allowed themselves to get all worked up on the voyage across the English Channel, others had a prayer meeting on deck and by the time the boat arrived in Folkestone the girl who had collapsed was completely recovered.

With Moses, we have to learn in theory *and in practice* that God is able to save, deliver, lead and provide. We have to prove God for ourselves. A diet of paperbacks which tell us of the remarkable faith of others is no use unless we begin to walk by faith in the same God. Our first steps in this faith-journey may be tentative and uncertain, but if there is faith on our part we shall find the Lord guiding those steps and strengthening our feet and our confidence in him. Remember, it is not great faith in God that we need, but faith in a great God.

Discussion Questions

1. How should we react to critical comment (especially from within the Church) of a faith project and its leaders?

2. In what circumstance may we attempt an "impossible" project, confident that God will make it happen?

3. How can we translate our faith from theory to practice?

4. Can you find examples of these principles from your own experience?

PART II
MOSES-MAN OF PRAYER

4
PREVAILING PRAYER

Effective Christian leadership seems always to be founded on three bases: faith, prayer and faithfulness (usually expressed as hard work).

One such leader in modern times was Lt. Gen. Sir William Dobbie, who was governor of Malta during World War II. A secular newspaper printed the following obituary: "His great personal courage, which he demonstrated by active leadership in rescue work during the raids on Malta, was harnessed to a passionate belief in the power of prayer. He read the Bible daily. He never deviated from the belief that divine mediation saved Malta. He deprecated the theory, advanced by most, that his own conduct and bearing, by inspiring others, had played no small part. He preferred to regard himself as an instrument."

Such a tribute would equally apply to Moses and to thousands of others leaders for God down through the centuries. Certainly the link between the fallible human being called Moses and the mighty man of God called Moses is the link of prayer—he had learned how to come to the Lord for help in

all circumstances. The walk of faith is impossible without a
life of prayer.

> Then came Amalek and fought with Israel at Rephidim.
> And Moses said to Joshua, "Choose for us men, and go out,
> fight with Amalek; tomorrow I will stand on the top of the
> hill with the rod of God in my hand." So Joshua did as Moses
> told him, and fought with Amalek; and Moses, Aaron and
> Hur went up to the top of the hill. Whenever Moses held up
> his hand, Israel prevailed. But Moses' hands grew weary;
> so they took a stone and put it under him, and he sat upon
> it, and Aaron and Hur held up his hands, one on one side,
> and the other on the other side; so his hands were steady
> until the going down of the sun. And Joshua mowed down
> Amalek and his people with the edge of the sword. (Exodus
> 17:8-13)

After the Lord intervened to deliver his people from Egypt
and then to provide for them in the wilderness, there came a
new challenge—a direct attack to halt their direct advance on
God's course. In our day, we can apply the lessons Moses
learned in many spheres of Christian activity where the
enemy's opposition is open and flagrant.

Prayer, a Substitute for Action?
Retreating to pray may, on the surface, appear to be a deeply
"spiritual" response. But it may really be only a convenient
way out of real involvement in the battle. However, if you
plunge impetuously into the fight without the preparation of
prayer (and therefore without dependence on the Lord) you
are heading straight for defeat! At Rephidim there was a clear
example of the balance between praying and fighting. It involved team work. The younger men were more capable of
hand-to-hand fighting and the older men to battle in prayer.
This is often the pattern in a church family where, though

everyone will be included in prayer and action, the younger people will take more of the heat of the work itself and the older ones will accept more of the responsibility of praying. It might be reasonable to assume that deepening levels of realistic prayer go hand in hand with deepening Christian maturity, and so it was Moses, Aaron and Hur who undertook this great responsibility.

Rod in Hand

Moses took in his hand God's rod. It was this which symbolized the deliverance from the power of Egypt. It had become a symbol, a wordless sign of the power of the Lord, a reminder to everyone who saw it of the victories already achieved for them by their sovereign God. Prevailing prayer has to begin in this way. It lays hold of the fact (and reinforces it in our own consciousness) that we are on the Lord's side, enrolled in the army of the God Who Is Victorious. This very day, as we come to him in prayer, we have a wide-ranging epic of biblical history from which to draw illustrations of his victory. This includes Egypt and the Red Sea, but supremely it includes the Cross of Jesus, his resurrection from the dead, the outpouring of his Holy Spirit and his transformation of eleven, timid, inexperienced followers into great leaders of this early church. The epic of historical Christianity also includes the growth and stabilization of the church and the welcoming of millions into the fellowship of his Son. This is our God, the one to whom we come in confident prayer.

On Top of the Hill

Why did Moses take his station at the top of the hill? Was it to encourage those who were battling it out in the valley? There was a time when I would have dismissed such an idea, insisting that prayer is to ask for results from God, not to encourage his followers.

Yet I know now just what an encouragement it can be to

know that others are supporting you in real prayer. I have
been deeply moved and helped by friends such as the little old
lady in a church I once served who told me, when I was visiting
there, "I pray for you every day." So it is with missionaries—
each one feels the need of constant support through prayer,
so when they are home on furlough they are blessed by the
knowledge that friends are clearly and faithfully standing
with them in prayer against the enemy.

There's another reason for standing on top of a hill. You get
such a marvelous view! From such a vantage point, Moses
would have been able to follow the movement of the battle
below in detail, seeing it more clearly than those who were
actually involved in the fighting. It was this which enabled him
to pray both accurately and specifically. Generalities such as
"Lord, bless the ones in battle" have little value. But a prayer
for Joshua over there at the front line, for the needs of the
company commanders, for those sections of soldiers most
under pressure at any given moment, for this weak spot in
the line and that counter-attacking force in trouble—that is
prevailing prayer. Battle prayer must be informed, up-to-
date. That is why it is often the people who are deeply involved in a work of God who carry the heaviest prayer
burdens, and who pray with the greatest conviction and with
the most astonishing results! It is noteworthy that when Jesus
wants to stimulate prayer for more workers for the harvest
field he asks his disciples to pray—the ones already busy
harvesting. After all, they understand the need better than
anyone else.

This is why it is easier for a church family to pray with
reality about matters affecting church life, witness and sur-
rounding needs. These are matters already on their hearts
and minds. It is not so easy to pray with such realism for
people with different ministries or for those serving other
countries about which we have only the vaguest (or inaccurate)
knowledge. Color slides and descriptive letters help, they

bring us closer, they give us more of a view from the hill, but there is nothing like first-hand experience, seeing conditions and needs for ourselves.

I felt this difference when I first visited Israel. I had seen many films and slide shows, but they only conveyed a fragmentary vision of what it was really like. We need to walk and smell and eat and shiver with cold or droop with heat as well as to see and hear.

What does this mean as far as "missionary prayer support" is concerned? I believe it means that those who have visited or served a part of the world will need to be the real pray-ers for that area. In these days of increasing world travel, I would encourage Christians to spend time, not only on the tourist attractions of a given country but investigating God's work there. We need to welcome ways in which enterprising missionary organizations are prepared to send out young people, even for a few months of service. Others may take the opportunity of academic studies in foreign countries, or working with the Peace Corps or with paramedical service organizations. All this will bring us closer to the action, providing us with information, the best fuel for prevailing prayer.

Keeping Informed
Not everybody can afford to travel. And we would be wrong to conclude that their prayers are therefore of less value. But they will need to supplement their general knowledge of missionary needs. How much more effective it would be if each of us, or groups of us, could give number one priority to one missionary in prayer, reading and learning all we can about current problems and circumstances in that missionary's area, informed by the missionary himself by letter or cassette so that we can pray frequently and specifically for the details of the battle. It isn't practical for a praying Christian to be informed and involved at this level with all sorts of different countries and missionaries. So many prayer letters come through the

mail. Are they really read and used or are they casually discarded with the junk mail?

Of course, this selectivity cannot apply to our church family as a whole. We have a responsibility to support all our missionaries in prayer and if we have a number serving abroad (or in our own country) the challenge is even greater for us to be informed and faithful. The more responsible prayer will be in small groups and in the church to which I belong, each of our fellowship groups has adopted a missionary. It becomes obvious when we are praying as a church family that the really informed and effective prayers for specific missionaries come from individuals in small groups.

Cause and Effect

When Moses lifted up his hands, Israel prevailed; when Moses lowered his hands Amalek prevailed. (Exodus 17:11)

At this crucial moment in his people's pilgrimage, God teaches them a lesson about prayer in clear-cut and visual terms. Prayer and blessing are directly connected, or "geared together." It is not that prayer will *always* be answered so quickly or dramatically, but experiences of this kind strengthen our faith in the power of prayer so that we can never be the same again. Often the experience is remembered much later when we may be going through the perplexity of unanswered prayer or unclear guidance. It seems that the Lord gives us these times of direct "gearing-in" so that in the future we will be able to step out in faith in the face of new obstacles.

In a church in which I served as a curate, Reigate Parish Church in Surrey, we were learning a great deal about praying together. One Monday morning I asked my vicar, Peter Baker, whether he would feel right about me preaching on healing on the coming Sunday evening. I explained the line I wanted to take and he happily agreed. That Wednesday he was suddenly taken ill with a perforated duodenal ulcer and rushed to the hospital. He was critically ill. The bleeding could not be stopped. Our church prayer meeting fell on Wednesday and with great love and concern our church family brought him to the Lord in prayer. During this time of intercession the bleeding stopped.

Then on Friday, the small son of Jimmy Liddon, a staff member of the Church Pastoral Aid Society working and living in our parish, was admitted to the hospital with meningitis. In response to Jimmy's urgent request I prayed for the child, anointing him with oil early Sunday morning. The child was absolutely motionless, seemingly on the brink between life and death.

So by the time I reached the pulpit on Sunday evening a lot had happened in this area of illness and divine healing since the Monday morning! After the sermon we had an extended time of prayer as a congregation, waiting in silence before the Lord there in the church. And it was at that very hour that the Lord chose to restore that little boy (now a man!) to health.

Why was the blessing of this answer so directly geared to the prayer? So much prayer for healing seems to bring inconclusive results. Why did God answer *our* prayers at *that* time? I believe that it was because our church family needed that special, specific encouragement—that God is at work on our behalf, and that he hears us when we pray. The whole week was a mighty boost to the prayer life of the church.

In Platt, Manchester, the Lord encouraged us in similar ways and first of all at the start of a faith-project. Our new curate, Robert Warren, came as a bachelor at a time when we did not have a curate's house. He did not last long in the singles scene and when Ann came into the picture and marriage was imminent we needed a house for them. A highly suitable one became available on the same street as the church, but we were not able to act quickly enough and it was sold.

Eventually we were sure it was right to go ahead and get a house and so I phoned the realtor. "Funny you should have called me this morning," he said. "That house in Platt Lane has just this minute been put back on the market—the purchaser couldn't get a mortgage." Clearly the Lord had kept the house for us until the day he knew we could proceed! We immediately went ahead with the usual surveyor's report and a building society was prepared to give the church a mortgage. We had almost no funds available except for a small amount put aside during the time when we had had no curate. The realtor called with the ultimatum, "You must finalize this today." And we needed another £100 just for the deposit!

The three of us on the staff were leaving for a quiet morning at a neighboring church. We talked it all over in the car and on our return went into my study and just laid it all before the Lord—simply that we believed the house to be his choice and we needed the £100 that day.

Later, after tea, my wife Myrtle suddenly said, "Oh, I forgot to tell you. Something quite unusual happened this morning. Miss Jones came to the door (this was actually at the very time we were praying) and as soon as I opened the door she blurted out "I want the church to have my Defence Bonds, *immediately*." "Oh, yes," I said. "And how much are they worth?" "£105!"

When we came to cash them we found that they had not been deposited for the full term, so there was a deduction necessary. Yes, it came to £5!

That house became our curate's residence. But that was just the beginning. The eventual result was far more profound. God was going to lead us out into ventures of faith in building for him which would bring in tens of thousands of pounds. That incident of the £100 was the key, God's token that we were to go forward.

The Lord encouraged us several times in similar ways as we grew in Manchester. He also allowed a similar seal of encouragement as our ministry ended there and we were about to move to London. Our penultimate Sunday was Gift Day, an annual event. We had set our target in exact figures because we knew precisely the cost of the items it was to cover. £2,325 was the target figure and it was agreed that the Parochial Church Council would meet on the Wednesday to decide on how to act in the light of the amount needed. That Sunday night far too much was happening in people's lives for us to worry about the Gift Day total. So it was not ready for announcement until after everyone had gone home. It was, in fact, somewhat short of the target amount, but only one or two people knew that. Money came in through Monday and Tuesday. On Wednesday, at 5:30 p.m. we went across to the hall for a farewell reception. The total received was £2,321— just £4 short of the target! We were gratefully surprised.

When we returned to the rectory for the council meeting there was a white envelope in the mail box. In the envelope were four £1 notes! We found out later that these were from a student who had been away for the weekend and, suddenly remembering that he had not contributed, he got on his bicycle and rode to the rectory to deliver his gift. As we began the council meeting, the target had been reached *exactly* —£2,325. The council sat in awe, worshipping the living God who at this crisis point of changing ministers was so clearly encouraging the church by this "directly geared" answer to prayer.

In the All Souls Church Building Project we saw similar incidents of direct encouragement from the Lord at various stages. One evening we prayed specifically for one obstructive local official who was causing us a great deal of trouble. He was promoted and transferred out of the district the very next day! Yet it is just such "cause and effect" solutions that encourage persistence in prayer when the answers are *not* immediately given and which encouraged us in that same project to pray persistently for one major aspect of our plan for two and a half years and then see the answer given just one day before the final deadline. If we want all answers to prayer on the spot, we will be disillusioned and disappointed. If we find in the direct answers a stimulus for persistent praying, we have learned the lesson God has in mind for us. Moses learned it.

Holding Up his Hand

The raising of the arms with palms upturned was the attitude of prayer. The Hebrew word used to describe it here is also used for exalting and praising God. The implication is that sustained prayer needs to include the element of praise. The same idea is evident in Colossians 4:2 where Paul exhorts, "Continue steadfastly in prayer, being watchful in it with thanksgiving." The work of prayer must begin with a time of praise and must be infused with the spirit of praise in order to send us on our way afterwards with expectancy. A prayer meeting that only *asks* will end up spiritually paralyzed. Long periods of corporate prayer—such as a three hour prayer session, a day of prayer, a night of prayer, can be wonderfully refreshing and effective if they are balanced on the Word, thanksgiving, praise and serious, practical petition.

As the disciples discovered in the Garden of Gethsemane, it is much easier to sleep than to pray. Prayer is hard work. It can also be a joy, a blessing, an exalting experience, but it is work. Sometimes people are heard to say, "I'm not coming to the prayer meeting tonight. I don't enjoy it." Or "I don't feel like it." If our Christian activity is gauged by the enjoyment it gives us we are certainly on the wrong track. We need to be committed to our prayer groups whether we *like* praying or not. It is vital to the life and health of the Christian community and its witness. Knock out the prayer meeting and you might as well shut down all other activity in Christ's name!

Let me be quite clear. I am not saying that praying together (or alone) is an onerous duty. It is, or ought to be, a great joy, a vital link with God, the vibrant hub of the church family's life. But this joy is a bonus, not the main purpose of prayer. If prayer does not result in exhileration, it does not really matter. In prayer, come first and foremost to do business with the living God. It will require concentration, oneness with others, a heart-longing for the Lord's answer to the prayers being offered and a deep awe at the privilege of conversing with our Father and of being partners in his work.

How to Prevail

When Moses prayed, Israel prevailed. The word means that they were "given strength, or increasing in strength." How did this work out? Was it in some general lift in morale throughout the forces of God as they were locked in battle, or was it worked out in specific terms of each fighting man being strengthened and assisted as he fought? I think it was probably the latter.

Apply this to the local church situation. Is prayer for God's grace and strength in the battle answered in general terms, or is it worked out in each member of the body being strengthened in growth and service and witness? Surely the latter. Paul seems to indicate this in Ephesians 3:16: "That he may grant you to be strengthened with might through his Spirit in the inner man," and his testimony in Philippians 4:13 is "I can do all things through Christ who strengthens me." I suggest then that if you are a member of a local church, you should pray for the strength of the Lord to flow through you and each other member, recognizing that the greatest witness in the neighborhood will come from ordinary Christians living in the grace and strength of God. Some members of the body are weaker than others and need special prayer; others appear to be quite adequate, already strong and fruitful, but they need prayer too, to maintain that strength.

We *expect* the first part of verse 11—Moses prays and Israel prevails. It is the second part of the verse that hits us unexpectedly. When Moses lowered his hand, Amalek prevailed. Is that right? Shouldn't it read instead "When Moses lowered his hand, Israel did not prevail"? That would seem fair and understandable. But no, the Scripture says that Amalek *prevailed,* was strengthened for aggressive effort. How slow we often are to realize the power of the enemy. How naive we are to think he will stand still if we do! When we expose ourselves in the weakness that results from prayerlessness—whether as individuals or as a church family—we open ourselves to the *advance* of the enemy. Prayer not only contains the enemy, it pushes him back. I think one of the greatest surprises we will have in heaven will be when we look back and see the strength of the enemy in the fight here and realize how seriously we underestimated him. "We wrestle" said Paul, "against powers . . . against the spiritual hosts of wickedness."

Yet in looking at some churches or fellowships you would never get that impression. They argue and divide over trivia, offend one another by petty selfishness or pride, act without vision and seem to go about their activities as if they were simply a human organization dealing with earthly concerns. I long to go into some churches and shout: "Wake up! There's a war on!" We are in a battle and if we do not open our eyes to the issues involved and begin to fight realistically with the spiritual weapons provided for the warfare we cannot prevail—but the enemy *will*. The truth depicted graphically in Israel's fight with Amalek needs to be grasped by us all.

So His Hands Were Steady

Prevailing prayer can be exhausting. Some people seem particularly gifted for long periods of intercession. Sometimes we are called to times of special prayer in our lives as we face a particular challenge and we are given special resources by the Holy Spirit for this kind of praying. In the pages of Christian biographies we read of such burdens driving people to prayer. We experience this in our own lives. Yet on the whole it seems more likely that prevailing power will be exercised in groups. That is how it was with Moses. He needed the support of Aaron and Hur. They were three gathered together, even if the main weight of the responsibility was on Moses.

When Jesus gave the model prayer he taught us to address "*our* Father." In Matthew 18 he says "If two of you agree on earth about anything they ask, it will be done for them by my Father in heaven. For where two or three are gathered in my name, there am I in the midst of them." Praying together gives us a corporate strength, a reinforced encouragement. Often one member of a group approaches the prayer need from one angle and another from a different and fresh aspect. We help one another in covering the subject completely as well as in the actual warm fellowship of praying together. Group prayer for vital needs is an essential aspect of our functioning together as members of Christ's body.

A few years ago I undertook an inquiry with a group of enthusiastic believers concerning their prayer life. They all valued times of being alone with God each day in personal devotional Bible study, prayer and commitment. But not one of them practiced any regular intercession for wider concerns—it was almost totally absent except in the prayer groups of the church, in which they took a leading part. It would have been easy to be critical of them, but on reflection it seemed right that they should come together for this time of intercession. It means that the prayer meeting of the church fellowship must be planned with great care and it may mean overhauling the church's whole program so that the prayer meeting is really central and can be given priority by the whole group.

Often when we are praying for someone in special need at All Souls Church prayer meeting, we picture ourselves as the four men bringing their friend on a stretcher. We may be a couple of hundred people but together we carry this person or this need to Jesus. There can be a true group identification with the subject of our prayers—particularly when the individual is known personally to most group members.

Take Acts 12:5 where the church was praying for Peter in prison. There must have been a sense of urgency about the gathering and we are told that "earnest" prayer was made to God for him. The word used in the Greek has the sense of laying hands on someone or stretching out the hands to him. Again this is a vivid picture of identification. The praying fellowship reaches out in prayer and identifies with the one for whom they are praying. There is a deep oneness and closeness, grounded in real *agape* love.

Earnestness does not necessarily imply a very emotional utterance, but it does mean reality and sincerity. Elijah is described in James 5:17 as one who prayed fervently. The Greek word means literally "with prayer he prayed." It does not mean some elaborate verbalization but rather absolute honesty and sincerity. The reality of such a prayer—even if it is a sacrifice of time and energy—is inspiring and liberating. It is inspiring because of the knowledge that together we are really meeting with the Lord; liberating because we have been able to come and place our needs at his feet—the one who is more ready to answer prayer than we are to pray, the one who is able to do far more than we ask or even think. So we may go on our way rejoicing in the privilege of belonging to the Lord and sharing in a real fellowship with his people, and with an eager expectation of all that he is going to do in answer to each time of prayer.

Let's be sure that each of us plays our part in the corporate prayer gathering so that in this fellowship together, whatever we face in the world, whatever storms break upon the church, whatever challenges we have to meet together and whatever ventures we are called to enter into for the Lord we may "keep our hands steady until the going down of the sun."

Discussion Questions
1. What are the basic ingredients of effective Christian leadership?

2. Some pray. Some act. How can these two factors be co-ordinated in a church. Are there any dangers to be avoided?

3. If God wills something to happen, why does he often make it conditional upon our praying? For whose benefit does he do this?

4. How can we make our group or corporate prayer more real, wider in its concerns and more closely identified with those for whom we pray?

5
THE PASSION
OF PETITIONING
PRAYER

On the morrow Moses said to the people, "You have sinned a great sin. And now I will go up to the Lord; perhaps I can make atonement for your sin." So Moses returned to the Lord and said, "Alas, this people have sinned a great sin; they have made for themselves gods of gold. But now, if thou wilt forgive their sin—and if not, blot me, I pray thee, out of thy book which thou hast written." But the Lord said to Moses, "Whoever has sinned against me, him will I blot out of my book. But now go, lead the people to the place of which I have spoken to you; behold, my angel shall go before you. Nevertheless, in the day when I visit, I will visit their sin upon them."

And the Lord sent a plague upon the people, because they made the calf which Aaron made. (Exodus 32:30-35)

Although intercessory prayer may, as we have said, normally take place in fellowship, there is also the place of personal petition and there are times, as in Exodus 32, where the burden has to be brought to the Lord by the individual believer because there are no others who can share it with him. For Moses as the ordained leader there was the clash here between what he clearly saw to be the vision of God for his people and the rather shallow response of the people, who seemed too easily swayed and turned away from the truth. When the attack came from outside, as with Amalek, it was easy for the people to stand and be called out to special levels of faith and action. But when the attack came from among the people of God themselves, it was far more difficult to tackle and the problem was compounded by the disunity it brought.

Organization—The Real Solution?

Administration had been a heavy weight on Moses, and his father-in-law, Jethro, had recommended, in Exodus 18:18 ff, the clearer teaching of God's laws and principles so that the people could discern the truth for themselves without bringing every minor cause of dispute to Moses for resolution. He also recommended the organization of the people into groups with a commander over a thousand and each thousand broken down into hundreds, fifties and tens, each grouping with its own leaders.

Moses accepted the plan and put it into action. It was practical, and in theory seemed acceptable. Many Christian organizations plan to handle the work load like this and large church congregations set out to break the numbers down into smaller groups with leaders and assistant leaders. The difficulty with all such organization is that it is dealing with people, not with an assemblage of inanimate objects. Moses was told to "choose able men from all the people, such as fear God, men who are trustworthy and hate a bribe." This he did, but all who follow such a pattern learn quickly that to support those leaders, train them, correct them when wrong, and replace them when necessary, is immensely demanding. Since any such system is only as good as its leaders, some groupings will be successful, some mediocre and some weak. At least

Moses' leaders were not liable to be transferred to some other area because of their jobs, as seems to be so often the case today!

Everything started well for Moses. He called the leaders (Exodus 19:7) and told them of the Lord's promise that if Israel obeyed his voice they would be his people and his special possession. The message was transmitted to the people and they responded fervently "All that the Lord has spoken we will do." The Ten Commandments were revealed and interpreted; the covenant was sealed with blood (Exodus 24) and Aaron, Nadab and Abihu, with the seventy elders, had the privilege of sharing the vision of God with Moses. It was a high peak of spiritual experience, commitment and promise. Moses felt he could go alone up into the mountain and confidently leave the people in the charge of such leaders.

Trouble

The time when everything seems to be going extremely well in a Christian church or work can become the moment of new danger. This has been demonstrated in the pages of Christian history. What happens? Is it a spiritual headiness that makes us act like gods—assuming that whatever we do must be right? Some bizarre things have been done by people who claim some super-spiritual experience—even flagrant immorality. Is their judgment affected?

Perhaps the sinful nature within us can pervert even a leadership role within the church. With subtlety we turn it to our own self-sastisfaction, using it to dominate or manipulate others. Judging from the way some Christians hang on to their offices in the church even when unable to fulfil them adequately, it is evident that often their motive is also entirely wrong.

Another root of leadership-warping comes from a lessening dependence upon the Lord and consequently an increasing confidence in our own strength, ability and judgment. We get so busy rushing about in "the Lord's work" that our times of prayer and dependence on him get fewer and fewer. The barrenness of a busy life is upon us and our leadership becomes a danger to the kingdom of God.

Popularity is another trap in a leader's path. It is natural that we want as many as possible to have confidence in us, but if our decisions are molded by the pressure of opinion we may lose the clarity of spirit-led leadership. It is not an easy path. To ignore the weight of public opinion can also be stubborn and wrong. What is always needed is a calm detachment that can weight the pros and cons in the light of the fuller picture which is normally available to us as leaders.

Aaron seems to have been a victim of crowd pressure and in spite of all that had only recently happened in his experience of God and his promises of commitment, he took a course of action that would have seemed unthinkable a few days before. Such is the fickleness of human nature—"Let him who thinks he stands take heed lest he fall."

Make Us Gods!

The making of the molten calf, the drinking and the sexual orgy that occurred were reflections of heathen idol worship and other customs which had influenced the Israelites back in Egypt and lay surprisingly near the surface of their lives in spite of all that God had done for them. The Lord described it as corruption, as a turning aside from the way he had commanded. (This is precisely what we say of our own generation and it has been said of many generations through the centuries.) When such things happen among the people of God it brings shame and the enemies of the Lord are quick to observe and publicize them (Exodus 32:25). Today's newspapers love stories about the immorality of a clergyman, the organist running off with the churchwarden's wife, or disputes and disagreements in church circles. We shudder as we read such reports, for we share the shame of the people of

God. We feel the wounds because the Lord is wounded and the whole body suffers.

Disappointment

Aaron must have been a bitter disappointment to Moses. His deputy, who had shared so deeply in the delivery from Egypt, was exposed in all his weakness and added to it by one of the feeblest excuses in history: "I threw this gold into the fire and out came this calf." His sin was worsened by the fact that he really gave religious encouragement and sanction to corruption and disobedience. Our hearts ache when we see some so-called Christian leaders in positions of responsibility doing the same today—twisting, adapting, even misquoting scripture to give some semblance of authority to what they are saying or writing but actually giving religious support to corrupt and atheistic thinking.

What is the difference between a Moses and an Aaron? Surely the key is submission *under* the authority of the word of God. Moses' authority derived from God and he lived to communicate God's word, to interpret it in day-to-day, practical terms and to work out his own life under its direction and authority. Aaron vacillated. Sometimes he was like Moses but just as easily he usurped the authority of the Lord and substituted his own authority, albeit with the appearance of religious integrity. It is a subtle distinction, but it can result in differences of belief and action that are separated by a great gulf. Judgment has to come in a situation of this sort and those who are loyal to the Lord, in spite of their weaknesses and failures, are given the opportunity to identify themselves in penitential re-commitment. "Who is on the Lord's side? Come to me." Those who come have to exercise the agonizing administration of judgment on those who do not come. Blessing and judgment were vivid and visible in the Old Testament.

Rendez-vous with God

In this atmosphere Moses came to God alone in petitioning

prayer. His heart must have been a turmoil of conflicting emotions. He had been with the Lord on the mountain and had been shown the Lord's pattern for Israel. The experience must have been spiritually exhilarating but physically exhausting. Then he was confronted with the situation in the valley which engulfed him with heartrending disappointment, the need for immediate action, the painful executing of judgment, and the feeling of agonizing shame over it all. A lesser man might well have given up under the apparent hopelessness of it all, but Moses was a man of prayer.

Passion of Prayer
It is the intensity of this prayer that leaps from the pages and burns into one's own heart. This man is pleading for atonement—for sin to be forgiven. He does not try to whitewash the situation. He calls sin "sin," but his whole approach is motivated by love. It is much easier to condemn than to forgive, to criticize than to encourage. A scolding sermon is easy to preach, but not often effective. Love has to surround us completely when we come to speak out and pray through situations like this. Do we really want people to be forgiven, or do we secretly harbor the hope that they "get what they deserve?" (That was Jonah's problem at Nineveh!) The church has been harmed by someone's actions or by rebellion of a group of people. Do we want to see them forgiven and restored? It is easy to respond "Of course we do"—but, honestly, *do* we?

One of our dangers as Christians is that as we learn more of the word of God and know him better we see issues more sharply and clearly, often in a stark black or white, even when the Bible itself has a touch of grey. It is all too easy to be quick to condemn and slow to understand.

Paul has to remind the Corinthian church of this in II Corinthians 2:6: "For such a one this punishment by the majority is enough; so you should rather turn to forgive and comfort him, or he may be overwhelmed by excessive sorrow. So I beg you to reaffirm your love for him."

Love—profound personal concern—is the vehicle of Moses' prayer. As he pleads for the Lord's forgiveness for his people he lays himself on the altar. If God will not forgive their sin, then, he says, "blot me, I pray you, out of your book which you have written."

The same passion is in the heart of Paul in Romans 9:2-3: "I have great sorrow and unceasing anguish in my heart. For I could wish that I myself were accursed and cut off from Christ for the sake of my brethren, my kinsmen by race." Of course, he knows he cannot be—he has just said that nothing can separate us from the love of God in Christ Jesus—but he speaks with a heart that bleeds for Israel, that longs for the glory of God rather than for personal prestige. Paul is following in the footsteps of Moses, for his heart is fired with the same love. Yet this passionate love is shown supremely in the heart of the Lord, and Moses and Paul merely reflect it. How often the Lord pleads with his people in the Old Testament record; and in the New Testament we see Jesus deeply moved with compassion as he sees the people as sheep without a shepherd or as he weeps over the stubbornness of his people in Jerusalem.

How much do we know of this deep, identifying love? Are we really concerned for the glory of God in the church? Are we so agonized by division and ungodly behavior that we are driven to our knees *in love*?

Then, what of our non-Christian relatives and friends? Are we concerned for them in such a way that we bear them on our hearts, longing for them to know reconciliation with God, and prepared to offer ourselves to be used as the Lord wishes on their behalf? We may be the only Christian on our street, in our place of work, in our tennis club. Who else will hold up our non-Christians in prayer? Who else will petition for them, bearing them in the heart in intense intercession for their conversion?

It is amazing what happens when we begin to pray for others in this way. In Manchester we divided the parish into four areas and those who lived in each of the areas were asked to make that their special spiritual concern. So prayer for neighborhoods and people living in them became part of our life together. Almost immediately after we began to pray like this a retired missionary living in the parish came to me almost open-mouthed one Sunday morning.

"You'll never guess what has happened," she said, "my next-door neighbor came out of the house this morning and said 'I'm coming to church.'"

She had never come before! I know that retired missionary was a great prayer warrior, and though I am sure she carried her next-door neighbor to the Lord on her heart with deep love, what happened was still a delightful surprise!

For Moses the outcome of the prayer was not so delightful. The Lord says that the blotting out in his book is something he does and will apply to those who have sinned against him. The Lord is over all and weighs all the circumstances. While there is no assurance that if we pray for our relatives and friends they will all come to Christ, this does not excuse us from the responsibility. It may demand much persistence in prayer for many years, or we may soon have the joy of seeing them come to Christ. The results must be in the Lord's hands.

The depth of Moses' passion in his petitioning prayer must surely challenge each of us. We need to pray for ourselves that the love of Christ may continue to fill us and flood our hearts, so that our times of petition, whether in private or in fellowship with others, will be *real*—not the mere reciting of items and needs like some shopping list, but the entrance into the holiest with names and needs written on our hearts in the ink of love from God.

Discussion Questions

1. What are the advantages and the dangers of dividing

congregations into groups? What are the needs of their leaders?

2. How should leaders react to the pressure of public opinion?

3. What are some danger signs for a successful church or fellowship?

4. How can we develop a true, deep and loving concern for those for whom we pray?

6
PERSONAL PRAYER

I do not believe anyone can be a mature and effective Christian leader who has not given top priority to personal prayer. Once this is neglected the rot sets in and though the outward form may stagger on for awhile the eventual result is emptiness and uselessness. It is obvious, and yet we can be so blind to it.

Jesus underlined the importance of our abiding in him and he in us. The closeness of this relationship is vital to a fruitful ministry. Yet how subtly we can let things slide. It involves a loosening of our personal discipline: the morning rush squeezing out any conscious commitment of the day to the Lord, the minister feeling he can rely on his preaching preparation and the Sunday worship, or any of us assuring ourselves that we are too busy to fit in this time alone with the Lord but that anyway we seem to be able to cope quite well without it. Sometimes it is a "super-spiritual" excuse: "I'm not under some legal bondage, I simply pray when the Spirit moves me." Obviously we will all differ as to what part of the day is best for us in our varied lifestyles, but the Lord is always ready to meet with us and it is vital to our Christian life that we place the highest importance on spending time with him as often as possible. Moses did.

> The Lord said to Moses, "Depart, go up hence, you and the people whom you have brought up out of the land of Egypt, to the land of which I swore to Abraham, Isaac, and Jacob, saying, 'To your descendants I will give it.' And I will send an angel before you, and I will drive out the Canaanites, the Amorites, the Hittites, the Perizzites, the Hivites, and the Jebusites. Go up to a land flowing with milk and honey; but I will not go up among you, lest I consume you in the way, for you are a stiff-necked people."
>
> When the people heard these evil tidings, they mourned; and no man put on his ornaments. For the Lord had said to Moses, "Say to the people of Israel, 'You are a stiff-necked people; if for a single moment I should go up among you, I would consume you. So now put off your ornaments from you, that I may know what to do with you'." Therefore the people of Israel stripped themselves of their ornaments, from Mount Horeb onward.
>
> Now Moses used to take the tent and pitch it outside the camp, far off from the camp; and he called it the tent of meeting. And every one who sought the Lord would go out to the tent of meeting, which was outside the camp. Whenever Moses went out to the tent, all the people rose up, and every man stood at his tent door, and looked after Moses, until he had gone into the tent. When Moses entered the tent, the pillar of cloud would descend and stand at the door of the tent, and the Lord would speak with Moses. And when all the people saw the pillar of cloud standing at the door of the tent, all the people would rise up and worship, every man at his tent door. Thus the Lord used to speak to Moses face to face, as a man speaks to his friend. When Moses turned again into the camp, his servant Joshua

the son of Nun, a young man, did not depart from the tent.

Moses said to the Lord, "See, thou sayest to me, 'Bring up this people'; but thou hast not let me know whom thou wilt send with me. Yet thou hast said, 'I know you by name, and you have also found favor in my sight. Now therefore, I pray thee, if I have found favor in thy sight, show me now thy ways, that I may know thee and find favor in thy sight. Consider too that this nation is thy people." And he said, "My presence will go with you, and I will give you rest." And he said to him, "If thy presence will not go with me, do not carry us up from here. For how shall it be known that I have found favor in thy sight, I and thy people? Is it not in thy going with us, so that we are distinct, I and thy people, from all other people that are upon the face of the earth?"

And the Lord said to Moses, "This very thing that you have spoken I will do; for you have found favor in my sight, and I know you by name." Moses said, "I pray thee, show me thy glory." And he said, "I will make all my goodness pass before you, and will proclaim before you my name *The Lord;* and I will be gracious to whom I will be gracious, and will show mercy on whom I will show mercy. But," he said, "you cannot see my face; for man shall not see me and live." And the Lord said, "Behold, there is a place by me where you shall stand upon the rock; and while my glory passes by I will put you in a cleft of the rock, and I will cover you with my hand until I have passed by; t en I will take away my hand, and you shall see my back; but my face shall not be seen." (Exodus 33)

Get Apart

Moses used to take the tent and pitch it outside the camp, far away from the crowd. If we can really get apart from the hurly-burly of life into some special place it can be a great help and blessing—whether it is into a special corner of the house, or out into the open air in the garden or a nearby park, or using a church building during our lunch hour. I realize how difficult it is for those who share rooms or have no private place in the building where they live. Some people are able to "shut out" the atmosphere around them; others are forced to find the answer to their need of quiet outside their living quarters. When we *do* have a choice of place it seems wise to get away from distractions of work, books, letters, newspapers, television and radio so that we can give ourselves to the Lord. Most of us are easily distracted and may need consciously to leave all the pressure of life "outside the room" for this special time, even if we bring those pressures to the Lord in prayer.

Meeting with Whom?

"The tent of meeting" is Moses' own name for the place. It signifies the attitude he had to these times in the tent. If we follow in his steps we will do well to relegate such descriptions as "quiet time," "time of prayer and Bible study" or "daily devotions" to second place in our thinking and put "meeting with the Lord" in first place.

The approach to the tent was with the desire to "seek the Lord" and for Moses the experience was one of intimate relationship: "The Lord used to speak to Moses face to face, as a man speaks to his friend." Here is a rich two-way relationship!

Moses received as well as gave; he heard as well as spoke; as he laid matters before the Lord so he understood the Lord's answer, the Lord's perspective and the Lord's purpose.

It takes some Christians a while to grasp this. If our meetings with the Lord are always short and routine there is no time to think things over with the Lord. The right process seems to be that we tell the Lord all about the problem and then ask him to shed his light on it. Quite often as we continue to meditate on it with him he brings some scripture to mind or helps us see some other aspect or factor that we have overlooked.

This often happens to a preacher who is burdened about a particular speaking engagement and cannot get peace of mind about how to approach it—especially when the subject is not defined. He may need to have a pencil and paper ready as he prays, for very often, before he gets off his knees, he will have been shown the passage to discuss and the main burden of what is to be said. Whenever that happens there is an evident sense of "rightness" as the message is given.

Receiving

During the All Souls Building Project there were many instances of this kind of "receiving." About five months before the actual contract was due to start we were at the stage of plans and contract bids. The final decision would not be made until all the bids were received and that would be only weeks before the starting of the building work. Some decisions could not wait until then. One was that we would need an underground cable for television relay from our temporary "home" in our other church to a supplementary building, for overflows. The Post Office needed six months to install it. The cost would be high. Should we take this step or not?

As I meditated on this dilemma the Bible in front of me was open at Mark 11:22-23: "Have faith in God. Truly I say to you, whoever says to this mountain, 'Be taken up and cast into the sea' and does not doubt in his heart, but believes that what he says will come to pass, it will be done for him." Did I believe? Had not God so clearly led us as a church to move forward on this project? Would he give us all red lights a few months later? It was for me a sort of crisis of faith. I laid hold of Mark 11 and immediately telephoned the Post Office to order the TV cable—it was a tangible expression of faith. The Lord had put his finger on that passage for me in answer to prayer.

Later on, when the project was actually under way, we had to face another big decision. We could no longer delay the rebuilding of the organ. The cost was colossal on top of all that we were already committed to with the main building project. We arranged a meeting for the whole church family to share the matter frankly and openly and to decide what to do. For me the burden was one of integrity. We had committed ourselves to the builder in financially binding contracts and as Christians our word of commitment had to be fulfilled. A large amount of the money was still to be given. Should we add to that with further financial commitment?

As I laid this heartache before the Lord and meditated on all that was involved, wondering how to face the church meeting that very evening, the telephone rang. I got up to answer it, carrying my Bible with me. After the telephone conversation I put the receiver down and glanced at the Bible open on my lap at a completely different place from before. My eyes caught the words—1 Kings 8:56: "Blessed be the Lord who has given rest to his people Israel, according to all that he promised; not one word has failed of all his good promise, which he uttered by Moses his servant." For Solomon the integrity was attached to the *Lord's* word, not man's. This clinched matters for me. Did I not believe the Lord had led us all this way? And if he was leading us to take this next step would he not see us through? If it was his way it involved *his* integrity—and that is as certain as eternity.

Danger!

Sometimes there are those who seem to think that the Lord is telling them things all the time. As a result their lives are erratic and unreliable. Although the actions the Lord "tells" them to do often have fruitless or disastrous results, they cannot see that this suggests a fault in their spiritual "receivers." If we are responding to the genuine leading of the Lord he will clearly confirm it as his way. On the other hand, if we proceed but find his presence is not with us, then we should stop at once and come back to him on our knees. Exodus 33:15 shows us how clearly Moses grasped this.

One Such Meeting

Having been shown (in Exodus 33) that Moses frequently went apart to be with the Lord, we are allowed to enter into the privacy and frankness of one such divine encounter. Moses comes still suffering the agony and heartache of the golden calf incident. He is tired and exhausted. He begins with the assurance of his call: "*You* said to me, bring up this people." Without the conviction of the Lord's call he would have given up, for the whole task was beyond his human resources. Physical opposition had been one thing but this spiritual malaise in his assistant leaders and the rest of the people was infinitely more serious.

Many a person called to leadership for God has knelt where Moses knelt. They feel swamped by the size of the task, disappointed by the fickleness of human nature even among Christians, unsure about which way to go, and spiritually drained. The one and only rock in the midst of this swamp is the rock of God's call.

In the Church of England, although the people to be ordained have been interviewed, selected by a board and trained in theological college for several years, they are still asked on the day of Ordination: "Do you trust that you are inwardly moved by the Holy Ghost to take upon you this Office and Ministration?" and a year later "Do you think in your heart that you be truly called?" The *call* is the anchor in the storm, the firm ground for our feet, the landmark to which we can constantly return.

By Grace We Come

The conviction of Moses' call is followed by the conviction of his right to come into the presence of the living God and to meet with him. This is based on two facts: "You said 'I know you by name' and 'You have found favor in my sight'."

The conditions are the same for us. We come as children of God, brought into his family by his tender love and mercy.

Instead of having to beg from a distant, mysterious God, we slip into our Father's presence and share everything with him. For us the "finding favor" is expressed in the Cross of Jesus and the free salvation we have received by his grace alone.

Yet this "right to come" must also remind us of the need to be cleansed and renewed day by day. When the believer allows known sin to obstruct his life and witness he is harming his relationship with the Father, dishonoring the body of Christ and grieving the Spirit. As the psalmist said (Psalm 66:18), "If I had cherished iniquity in my heart the Lord would not have listened." Personal and corporate prayer should always begin with this consciousness of our need of forgiveness and of cleansing even from secret faults.

Asking

Moses' prayer centers on two petitions: "Show me your ways" and "Show me your glory." They are splendidly inclusive requests and each could be a helpful focus for personal prayer.

"Show me your ways"

Moses said, "Show me *your* ways": rather than "This is what *I* want." Moses' personal prayer is in the context of the plan and purposes of God. We need to see our whole lives within this context—our studies, our work, our career, our recreation, our Christian activities, our personal relationships, our ambition, our use of money, our attitude to possessions and security, the use of our mind, the development of our talents and our whole lifestyle. The prayer "Show me your ways" is wide enough in scope to include everything! And the proof that God answered this prayer is found in Psalm 103:7: "He made known his ways unto Moses."

But on this occasion Moses is not going to rise from prayer with the next stage of God's plan clearly revealed to him. Instead, God's answer is in terms of the divine guarantee, "My presence will go with you and I will give you rest." Moses may not see the next stage, but he can be assured that he is still on God's track and that the *direction* is right. This was the path laid out for him. To jump off it without the conviction that God is calling him off it would be to step out of the Lord's purposes.

Moses responded with the heart-cry, "If your presence will not go with me, do not carry us up from here." Note the personalization: "with *me*." Here the leader is deeply conscious of the enormous responsibility resting upon him as the servant of the living God. The one thing that matters is that he is in the Lord's path and that the Lord is with him. He knows, as we all must, that without the Lord he can do nothing.

Yet he also sees the importance of the Lord's presence, strongly reflected among the people of God. How else, he says, will outsiders see any difference? When God's people are really within his purpose, and his presence is manifestly upon them, it is an undeniable evidence to the unbelievers. As they see individuals of all sorts and conditions being united in love they know that this could never happen in a merely human context. As they see the people of God launching out in faith and the impossible becoming the possible, they know that this is not accomplished simply in human strength. Zephaniah echoed this certainty: "The Lord your God is in your midst; his power gives you victory." (Zephaniah 3:17) It is the obvious presence of the Lord in our midst that should distinguish every church congregation/family, and every Christian group of any kind. It should be the evident mark of every mission center and of every Christian committee, every spiritual hierarchy and administration. *Is the Lord in the midst?* Those who, from the heart, bring their work and life to the Lord, crying, "Show me your ways," will know that he is.

"Show me your glory"
The other part of Moses' personal prayer is a hungering to know more of the Lord. How often is that a part of our prayer?

It was a burden in the prayer life of Paul for himself and for his converts. In the famous prayer of Ephesians 3:14 he pleaded that they might know more of Christ and his love and of the fulness of God. A comment made some years ago about preaching arrested me: "Don't preach so much about *how* we should respond to the Lord but rather preach more of the Lord to whom we should respond."

How did God show Moses his glory? He certainly gave Moses an indescribable experience. Moses was to be in the cleft of the rock as the Lord revealed himself to Moses' physical eyes. It was to be an overwhelming and memorable event. However, the experience was not to be continuous—it came, and then it was over. Like the disciples on the Mount of Transfiguration centuries later we may want to stay in heaven while on earth, but there is work to be done—the special manifestations of God and mountain-top experiences of his majesty and love are to renew us in his service in the mundane realities of living.

When working in Nottingham in my first curacy we saw a young man won to Christ by being challenged on the street by a Christian. He was a tough, illiterate lad. After a while he went away for a holiday at a Christian retreat center. It was simply marvelous for him. When he came back he said, "It was like heaven—and coming back here is like hell!" We knew what he meant! The glorious times at retreats and conventions, when we meet with the Lord in a new way, are times to treasure and savor, but we cannot *live* there. We have work to do. Those who want to be on the mountain-top all the time end up by creating pseudo-spiritual experiences by the energy of the flesh and become useless as servants of Christ in the world.

There is something much more lasting about God's revelation of his glory. It is to be in terms of his goodness and mercy. These can be seen day by day—starting with ourselves. In the midst of the most pagan surroundings we can see the Lord at work in people's lives. Here the glory of the Lord is being demonstrated. We see the Lord's overruling of circumstances, his answers to prayer, his light shining in dark places, his triumph in the lives of martyrs, his victory and peace in the midst of suffering, his opening of blind eyes that they may see him. Time and time again we cry, "This is the Lord's goodness; this is his mercy—Hallelujah!" So, though special experiences of his glory may come and go, we must say with the psalmist, "Surely goodness and mercy shall follow me *all* the days of my life."

Lord, Show Us Your Ways; Show Us Your Glory
Much was about to happen. The people were about to share and cooperate in a thrilling way. People with gifts of workmanship and other talents would come forward willingly to help. The people would start giving of their possessions with such enthusiasm that they would need to be restrained from giving more (Exodus 36:6) and when the tabernacle was made the glory of the Lord would fill it (Exodus 40:34). But the key to it all was back in the tent of meeting—Moses alone with the Lord, laying his heart open and receiving the Lord's encouragement and confirmation.

No wonder Moses' face shone (Exodus 34:29). And his experience may be ours! "We all, with unveiled face, beholding the glory of the Lord, are being changed into his likeness from one degree of glory to another; for this comes from the Lord who is the Spirit". (II Corinthians 3:18)

There are always new levels of prayer to be discovered as we go on in our Christian lives, new understandings of his ways, new reasons for praise, new areas in which to see the Lord at work, new circumstances in which to prove him. So Moses' own testimony at the end of his life was "There is none like God, who rides through the heavens to your help, and in his majesty through the skies. The eternal God is your dwelling place and underneath are the everlasting arms" (Deuteronomy 33:26-27). And the final verdict of the Pentateuch as to the key to Moses' greatness was this: "There was not arisen a prophet since in Israel like Moses, whom the Lord knew *face to face*." (Deuteronomy 34:10) Moses was a man of prayer.

Discussion Questions

1. What are the early warning signs of spiritual slackness? How can we protect ourselves in this area?

2. How can we know whether God is speaking to us, or we are following our own ambitions and desires?

3. How should we react to a situation in which only the next stage of a faith project has been revealed to us, and the final outcome remains hidden?

PART III
MOSES–MAN OF FAITHFULNESS

7
FAITHFUL
IN THE CONVICTION
OF THE
LORD'S PRIORITY

After major victories of faith and action it is often quite difficult to cope with the "going on," dealing with smaller issues
that can often seem enlarged all out of proportion. Faithfulness has to find the balance between faith and prayer.
Moses was someone the Lord could trust (Numbers 12:7).
It may seem a simple thing to be trustworthy, but any Christian leader knows that one person who can be relied upon to
carry through a work is worth ten who approach Christian
work casually. Jesus "was *faithful* to him who appointed him,
just as Moses was *faithful* in God's house" (Hebrews 3:2). Our
minds will readily recall the accolade of Matthew 25:21, "Well
done, good and *faithful* servant," or the question of Luke
12:42, "Who then is that *faithful* and wise steward?" or the
statement of I Corinthians 4:2 "It is required of stewards that
they be found *faithful*."

It is a regrettable fact that some Christians regard "success" in terms of numbers and size. The Bible sees it in terms
of faithfulness. Faithfulness may mean a lifetime of sowing
without observable results while another may reap a full

harvest; it may mean working away in an unseen corner of the
Lord's vineyard or being exposed to the limelight, but whatever or wherever the job, the Lord requires faithfulness. Can
he trust us where we are now?

There are many examples of that faithfulness worked out
in the life of Moses as he led the people on through the wilderness. Let us look at some of them and apply their lessons to
ourselves.

Lordship

Who is Lord? The issue of the Lordship of Christ in our lives
is one to be faced and worked out in every Christian's experience. The response to Jesus as Savior can be a very self-
centered thing if it is not matched by openness to Christ as
Lord. We can "use" Jesus, receiving the benefits of salvation,
rather like Social Security or insurance benefits. In such a
case Jesus is on the periphery with other people and things,
there to serve and keep and benefit *us*. It is a very comfortable form of Christianity—if it can be called "Christian." Jesus
will be there to be prayed to for security of home and job and
family; to give us a warm feeling each Sunday in church; to
comfort us in sorrow and to be a safe refuge at death. If anything in church life or work disturbs our comfort, we are
upset. If we are not benefiting from the fellowship, we complain—isn't it there for our benefit? If the church develops a
concern about social justice or service or starts demanding
sacrificial giving and costly faith, we move elsewhere. Such
"Christianity" on our part is next to worthless.

The paradox of Christianity is that it is both comfortable
and uncomfortable at the same time! Our times of worship
and study of the Word should bring peace to our souls and
action to our lives. We should be both calmed and stirred;
secure and convicted; refreshed and recommitted; conscious
of our blessings and aware of our failings; glad to glory in the
Cross as the means of our salvation and ready daily to take up

the Cross and follow Christ, whatever the cost. With many who come to faith in Christ this double aspect is consciously present at once. Some others need a spiritual revolution to stir them from merely self-centered Christian living. They need the dynamite of the Holy Spirit.

Priority of the Lord's Will

On the day that the tabernacle was set up, the cloud covered the tabernacle, the tent of the testimony; and at evening it was over the tabernacle like the appearance of fire until morning. So it was continually; the cloud covered it by day, and the appearance of fire by night. And whenever the cloud was taken up from over the tent, after that the people of Israel set out; and in the place where the cloud settled down, there the people of Israel encamped.... Whether it was two days, or a month, or a longer time that the cloud continued over the tabernacle, abiding there, the people of Israel remained in camp and did not set out; but when it was taken up they set out. At the command of the Lord they encamped, and at the command of the Lord they set out; they kept the charge of the Lord, at the command of the Lord by Moses. (Numbers 9:15, 16, 22, 23)

One important lesson for the Christian to learn is that he is a pilgrim, with no fixed abode here. If the Lord's will has priority in his life he will be constantly ready to change course or, like the soldier, ready for fresh orders. Our readiness to think and act in quick obedience when security can so often be in materialistic terms is not automatic. Paul tells Timothy (2 Timothy 2:4) "No soldier on service gets entangled in civilian pursuits, since his aim is to satisfy the one who enlisted him." If the Lord's will is our goal, our objective, the obeying is much easier.

In Numbers 9:15-23 there is a clear illustration of this truth. The Lord guides his people by the cloud and the fire. It was a very visible form of guidance—we all prefer guidance in plain, unmistakable terms! But the very clarity of the guiding signs meant that there was no doubt when they were to move on or to stay—there was no possibility of misinterpreting the guidance signals!

Don't Put Down Roots!

The point of this passage is in the "restlessness" of the Lord's leading. The Israelites had to live with the daily possibility of moving on (Numbers 9:21). Sometimes they stayed just a night—hardly worth unpacking for. Or it could be a two-day stop (v. 22) or encampment for a month, or a longer time. They could never be sure. They could never afford to get so settled that they could not move quickly when the moment came. They were pilgrims.

So is the believer today. For him to say "I am in this job and settled in this house until retirement" is to deny his pilgrim status. He *may* stay there until he dies, but he should never count on it. Throughout his life he needs to ask God, "Do you want me to move on?"

Sometimes, of course, it is harder to stay where we are—we long to move, but the cloud settles in one place. We wish we could go off to Africa to serve God but instead, here we are, cooped up in a small city apartment and it looks like we're here for life. We can feel hurt, and neglected. A spirit of resentment can come in, unless clearly we have the Lord's priority at the center of our lives and can grasp afresh that *faithfulness where we are* is what he wants. If we smother in self-pity we can become quite useless. People who have soured, who always think the grass is greener on the other side of the fence, are invariably useless in the service of God and his church.

God's Time-keeping

This passage also teaches us to trust the Lord's *timing*. We are often in such a hurry. People in training at Bible or theological college have been known to throw up their studies and go off. They "cannot wait to get on with the Lord's work." They are seldom heard of again. It is good, in the urgency of youth, to remember that the Lord Jesus did not begin his public ministry until he was thirty years of age—but how richly prepared he was for that ministry! We may need much more training than we are prepared to admit and that will mean submission to the unwelcome discipline of more study or wider experience. Such submission is part of faithfulness.

We also get restless at apparent delays in the working out of some task for the Lord. Why is it not happening *now?* Why is that blockage allowed? Why is that circumstance not overruled? If we are sincerely taking the matter to the Lord in prayer we must believe that there is a far greater purpose in the delay than we can see. The Lord can see the whole picture —we can only ever see a tiny part of it. Later as we look back we can see why things happened as they did—and then we will praise him.

One of my favorite publications is a bus schedule! I am fascinated by the way all the different connecting routes are fitted together. Delays at some bus terminals are deliberately planned to allow non-stop trips or to make connections. Yet even on the best-run bus lines there are the unexpected delays. Air travellers experience even more of this kind of delay, sometimes on the ground, sometimes circling while waiting clearance to land. We never like sitting in a bus or a plane, seeing the minutes tick by in delay but we know that if the driver or pilot proceeded under his own authority a major disaster could occur. We know that someone, somewhere, sees the whole picture and is acting in the most efficient way. So it is with the Lord.

Under the Lord's Command
No verbal command is spoken by the Lord—simply the sign of

cloud or fire. Yet Numbers 9:23 says, "At the command of the Lord they encamped and at the command of the Lord they set out." There are many ways in which God guides, and we have to be careful not to restrict our ideas of his guidance to one particular method. Six months after I had the shock of believing God was calling me into the ministry, I was still seeking confirmation of that call. I wanted to be absolutely convinced. Late one night I was reading a comment of Oswald Chambers' on Isaiah 6. Effectively for me he pointed out that "God did not address the call to Isaiah; Isaiah *overheard* God saying—'who will go for us?' Get out of your mind the idea of expecting God to come with compulsions and pleadings." That is what I wanted—some angelic being, some blazing message, some *certainty*! But, as he pointed out, if we are called of God we simply hear the still small voice questioning, all the time, "Who will go for us?" I had been limiting God's ways of guidance and I realized that the insistent conviction of the call that had gone on for more than six months was indeed God speaking. I needed no other sign or word. I knelt in adoration and said, "Here am I, send me."

I have found this to be true in many others' experience. One young man considering the church ministry came to see me one day. "I'm told by my minister and friends that it is right to go ahead. All the circumstances are fitting together, I have a real inward conviction about it, but I am just waiting for a word from the Lord. *Then* I'll go!" He meant some word of Scripture. But he did not need it. God had already written it plain and clear!

Guidance seems to get less clear for some Christians as they get older—perhaps that is the mark of growing maturity in the faith. We should not need it to be written quite so plainly. But we do need to learn that God's ways of guidance vary and that even inward conviction can be missing if we are too deeply involved emotionally in the place where we are at that time. It is something of the entanglement of II Timothy 4.

Usually there will be guidance by inward conviction *or* circumstances, or by the advice of others *or* by a direct word of Scripture. Sometimes in at least two ways—or more.

Let me illustrate from railways and signalling. Two yellow lights encourage the driver to go on with more confidence—at least two sections are clear. Green means proceed at full speed. It is a fair rule-of-thumb about guidance in terms of the four main ways mentioned above. Yet the Lord of our lives is not restricted by any of them and if we deeply desire his will and way he will show us whatever way he uses and we shall say as Moses did: "At the command of the Lord we encamped and at the command of the Lord we set out."

Priority of the Lord's Worth

In Numbers 11 we read how Moses was constantly under attack about "things"—ordinary things, like food and comfort. It is true that we do not know how much we value things until we lose them. As a student I was responsible for getting a large party of boys to camp. The journey was long and rather complicated but finally we arrived at the Devon railway station and half-an-hour later at the camp site. All the luggage was collected. The responsibility was over. I looked for my own case. It was not there! It had in it almost all of what I possessed in those days and I was thrown off balance by the loss. It actually turned up the next day—it had been thrown off at an earlier station—but not before I had learned, to my surprise, how much I valued things. It is no surprise that Israel reacted as they did, though it was still inexcusable.

"The people complained about their misfortunes." How easily the deliverance from oppression was forgotten. "Oh that we had meat to eat! We remember the fish we ate in Egypt for nothing, the cucumbers, the melons, the leeks, the onions and the garlic; but now our strength is dried up and there is nothing at all but this manna to look at." They all wept for meat! As Acts 7:39 puts it, "In their hearts they turned back again into Egypt." They chose to forget the taskmasters, the making of bricks without straw, their desperate cries for deliverance! Our human memories have a convenient way of selecting what they want to remember. Yet the awful thing about this incident was the way in which they despised the manna. Without it they would have been dead. True, it was the same thing every day, cooked the same way, but it was still God-given and life-sustaining. Every day's fresh supply should have been a cause of praise and thanksgiving: "New every morning is your love."

Tired of the Same Old Thing?
We need to be reminded of this lesson. A similar spirit of tiredness can occur in a Christian community or church fellowship. We may have the same sort of program each week, similar services, the same preachers, the same people, the same diet of worship or teaching and the same work of evangelism to be done. Humanly, we feel driven to demand some variety, some special excitement, something extraordinary rather than this "manna" every week. (However I must hasten to affirm that ordinary church worship and Christian activity need not be dull or boring!)

Of course, much of the life of the Christian church *is* the same, because it is feeding on the same Lord, and working out what it means to be in the same Body. This "sameness" may be seen as a matter of joy and praise, a cause for thankfulness. The center of our worship is at the Lord's Table and here we joyfully celebrate our deliverance Sunday by Sunday. Let us not be fooled into thinking that life is really more attractive or exciting outside Christ! The glorious privileges that are ours as members of the Lord's family are overwhelming.

One Decisive Lent
For many people this conflict between hankering for the past and rejoicing in the present has to be fought out in a decisive

battle. The late Alan Stibbs, a great expositor of the Scriptures, used to say that in his life there had been "one decisive Lent" when he thrashed out the principles and priorities of his life. He then lived them out for the rest of his life. The missionary or minister may find himself hankering after the salaries and standards of living he sees in his contemporaries in secular occupations. It will go on being a matter that gnaws at the heart unless there is a "decisive Lent" when the principles of the Lordship of Christ and his supreme value over all else this world can offer are thrashed out and established once and for all.

Moses must have sorted this out more than anyone else on that great pilgrimage. He had experienced the luxurious living of Pharaoh's household and had known privileges greater than free fish and garlic. Hebrews 11:24-26 expresses it thus: "By faith, Moses, when he was grown up, refused to be called the son of Pharaoh's daughter, *choosing* rather to share ill-treatment with the people of God than to enjoy the fleeting pleasures of sin. He considered abuse suffered for the Christ greater wealth than all treasures of Egypt, for he looked to the reward." Moses sorted out his life priorities at this critical point. Jesus expects us to get sorted out, too. The latter part of Matthew 6 puts the issue clearly. Things—material possessions—are relatively unimportant. Certainly we should not worry about them, but "seek first God's kingdom and his righteousness, and all these things will be yours as well."

Saturation

How did God deal with the people? He did the opposite of what one might expect. He sent *meat* (Numbers 11:19-20), not for one day, or ten, but for a whole month, "until it comes out of your nostrils and becomes loathsome to you." It was an effective teaching method! Often one finds young Christians who want an ice cream Christianity rather than a bread one. Like spoiled children they refuse to feed on the bread of the Word but rush from one sundae "happening" to another, reveling in them until eventually they are nauseated by their emptiness and superficiality. In the mercy of God one trusts that then they learn to hunger for the true bread rather than drop away from the faith altogether.

It is seldom much use reasoning with someone who has set his heart on the ice cream existence. He will regard you as dull, fuddy-duddy, or even unspiritual. He has to get sick of it before he will listen.

So it was there in the wilderness. Only when the Israelites started loathing the very thing they craved for did they see that what they had been doing with their complaining was to reject the Lord. For that was the issue. Was being with the Lord, as part of his people—being led by him and fed by him —worth everything else? Did they believe in the worth-ship of Jehovah?

Job had to learn that lesson the hard way. And Habakkuk expresses his conviction of the Lord's worth-ship in those marvelous words: "Though the fig-trees do not blossom, nor fruit be on the vines . . . Yet I will rejoice in the Lord, I will joy in the God of my salvation." Paul was prepared to count "all things as loss" for the excellency of knowing the Lord. The disciples left everything to follow Christ. Is the Lord worth everything to us?

Discussion Questions

1. In practical terms, what does it mean for a Christian to be constantly ready to change course at God's bidding?

2. What principles of guidance does God use to lead an individual or a Church?

3. Has your Church or fellowship become stale and tired? If so, what can be done about it?

8
FAITHFUL
IN THE CONVICTION
OF THE
LORD'S CALLING

The sure conviction of the Lord's calling was a turning point for Moses at several times in his life—we have seen it in the early days and in his personal prayer at Sinai. It was tested in the wilderness journey in several different ways. Once again we must emphasize the importance of the assurance of God's call in any work for him. We will be forced to look back and reaffirm it many times and the test of it will come even through unexpected events.

People who are unsure of themselves or their vocation can be very defensive about their position and react by being critical of or unsympathetic to the position of others. They may seek to bolster their own security by running down potential opposition. This can become a vicious and malicious activity, with jockeying for jobs, currying of favors, character assassination by innuendo and warped rumor. In Christian circles it can even be spiritualized, to gain a spurious acceptability.

Somebody Is Out of Line?

The gathering of the seventy (Numbers 11:24) was marked by a special touch of the Lord, as the Spirit rested on them and they prophesied. It happened for a time and then the prophesy ceased. There were two men who, for some reason, did not go out to the tent—Eldad and Medad. The Spirit rested on them, too, as part of the seventy, and they prophesied but only in the camp. This caused quite a stir. One young man was sent running to tell Moses, and Joshua was all for forbidding them.

But Moses answered "Are you jealous for my sake?" *Why*, he asked, are you upset about it? What is really causing your reaction? Is it a form of jealousy? Or a wrong view of authority? Moses had no doubt that they should have rejoiced at seeing these two men prophesy, rather than complain. He longed that the Spirit might inspire and bless all the Lord's people. Because he did not feel threatened by the event, he could assess it with a clear eye to the real spiritual issues.

Paul has the same clear eye in Philippians 1:17. As he sits in prison he hears of those who are preaching Christ from envy and rivalry. He comments: "They proclaim Christ out of partisanship, not sincerely, but thinking to afflict me in my imprisonment."

I ask myself—how I would react in such circumstances? I think my natural reaction would be indignation—but not Paul! He rejoices that "whether in pretence or in truth, Christ is proclaimed." It is an amazing reaction and springs from the heart of someone who knows his calling, does not feel personally threatened by others who fulfill a similar calling and who can see through the surface concerns to the real issues. There would be other situations where a study of the real issues would cause Paul to disapprove of or forbid something. Then the right approach would be to analyze and expose the falsity. To Moses' mind, the touch of the Spirit had been upon the seventy, not just upon the two, and was therefore gen-

uinely of the Lord. For Paul, the preaching was about Christ
—hence he could rejoice. If the proclamation had been anti-
Christ or had mocked the truth he could not have rejoiced in
the same way. It is not simply a matter of tolerance but of
asking whether the Lord is in this thing or is being uplifted
by it. If he is not, we must gently but firmly oppose it.

Jealousy

Clearly Moses is not jealous for his reputation. "Are you
jealous for my sake?" Would to God such an attitude was characteristic of every Christian worker! How easily jealousies
can arise and in some Christian communities the atmosphere
has been ruined by the sort of pettiness that ought to have
been left behind in kindergarten. Tragically, it can occur any-
where. The root of jealousy often lies in an uncertainty of our
calling from the Lord. We fail to grasp what it means to be
secure in the Body of Christ, where the Head of the Body
assigns to us different functions and equips us appropriately.

When another person in the church seems to win many to
Christ and we do not, we can feel miserably jealous of their
success instead of rejoicing in their particular evangelistic
gift. Someone else is called to missionary work overseas. Their
name gets included on the church prayer diary. They have
the new status of "missionary," complete with a valedictory
service, travel to a far country, special prayer support in the
church at home, and a great deal of attention when they come
home on furlough. And we are stuck right here, teaching,
perhaps, in a tough school where there is little if any real
Christian fellowship and support. We are not featured and
feted. It is natural that we feel jealous, though we would not
admit it.

King Saul had a problem of jealousy. When the women
started singing that though Saul had slain his thousands,
David had accounted for tens of thousands, he threw a javelin
at David to kill him. Perhaps the rector of the church hears all

around him, "The curate preaches much better than the rector." That is not easy to take! Or perhaps you have been occupying the piano stool at Sunday School for 20 years—it has become your "right" as well as your place of service. You prize it—secretly of course! Then along comes this much younger Christian who has a far wider musical training, who could do all sorts of creative musical things with the children. Do you hand over? Or do you dig in your heels and find reason to criticize "these young things and their modern ideas?" Is it the best for God that we want, or the best for ourselves? Faithfulness in God's calling means appreciating gladly and freely the calling of others, and rejoicing in what they are doing for the Lord.

Leadership Crisis

No sooner had Moses coped with the Eldad and Medad "threat" than he had to face a direct attack from his two assistant leaders—Aaron and Miriam (Numbers 12). The real point of their attack was hidden at first. They criticized him for marrying a Cushite woman. But the real issue was over his leadership. Leaders have to learn to discern what lies behind a criticism or attack. Is it the critic's own anxieties that are being worked out under the guise of some apparently spiritual attack? Is what is being said in criticism the real issue or is there something deeper which is causing it? Usually there is. It now comes out: "Has the Lord indeed spoken only through Moses? Has he not spoken through us also?" Attacks from your colleagues, your staff, your council or committee, are probably more hard to hear than from others. The first thing to ask ourselves is "Are the criticisms justified?" We can be over-protective of our position, but open sharing within a staff team should mean that direct criticism is unnecessary— we can learn from one another far better in loving openness and fellowship.

Silent Response

How does Moses meet this attack? It seems he met it with

silence until the judgment of Miriam when, in love, he pled for her healing. Our Savior showed us the majesty of silence as he was accused, insulted and goaded at his "trial." I had to learn my first lessons in this soon after I was ordained. One Tuesday morning I received a letter from two ladies in the church in which I was more or less told I was unfit for the ministry—the sermon I had preached on the Sunday night would have put them off Christianity forever if they had been simple enquirers and not more "mature" Christians. Their critical comments filled page after page. I felt hurt, wounded and angry. After all, several people had told me they had been especially helped through the sermon. I went to show the letter to my vicar.

"Michael," he said, "you must write a soft answer that turns away wrath."

"But I can't!" I exclaimed, exasperated.

"You must," he said.

It took me all day to find ways of writing a "soft answer." The next Sunday the ladies ignored me. The following week as I arrived at the gate of the church grounds for the prayer meeting there they were. I could not run away. They stepped forward. "Mr. Baughen . . . do let me carry your bag!" So this young curate found himself having his attaché case carried up the path by two older ladies. My vicar was right!

Later on in my life I found myself caught in the middle of cross-fire over the future of a theological college. All sorts of unfair, distorted and grossly inaccurate things were written and verbalized in the heat of the argument. In such a situation the only course for me was one of silence. To have tried to justify myself would have been of no avail. But it still hurt— very deeply. Most of us are at least able to share with others when such attacks come, and receive loving wisdom and support. Moses had to take it alone.

Vindication by the Lord
Silence on Moses' part allowed the vindication of God to be

crystal clear. The Lord declared his calling of Moses and his sealing of him in this special leadership role. Moses is more than a prophet—"He is entrusted with all my house," said the Lord, "With him I speak mouth to mouth clearly and not in dark speech." Aaron and Miriam, in their jealous outcry, had therefore spoken against the Lord's calling and designation of Moses. He had been clearly set apart by God. So "Why then were you not afraid to speak against my servant Moses?"

It is a salutary shock to realize that easy criticism of others may well be criticism of the Lord who called them. Judgment came for Miriam in the form of leprosy. Aaron, as High Priest, would have had to declare her a leper—almost worse for him than suffering the disease himself. Aaron confessed their sin and foolishness but Miriam had to be excluded from the camp in shame for seven days.

Thus there was heartache, the fellowship was wounded, the leadership had been weakened, and the cloud of the Lord was removed from the tent. In exactly the same way, divisions and disputes among members of churches and staff teams virtually bring blessing to a stop. How necessary it is that we "endeavor to keep the unity of the Spirit in the bond of peace" —for the kingdom's sake as well as our own. Quick action can often prevent worse damage. The injunction not to let the sun go down on our anger (Ephesians 4:26) is so that we "give no opportunity to the devil." The exhortation to loving forgiveness in the fellowship in II Corinthians 2 is "to keep Satan from gaining the advantage over us; for we are not ignorant of his designs." If Satan can split our fellowship he has won a major victory.

Yet Again—and Even More So!

A third attack was to follow on Moses' leadership. You would think everyone would have learned the lesson by now, for everyone had had to wait until Miriam was received back into camp. But no! In Numbers 16 Korah led a rebellion. He organized it well, bringing with him two hundred and fifty leaders from the congregation, well-known men chosen from the assembly. It would be interesting to know if some of these leaders had nursed a grievance at not being included in the seventy elders selected when the Spirit was given!

Selecting people is always dangerous. I dislike our annual parochial church council elections. With more nominations than places, there are bound to be losers in the vote, and even the most self-effacing person can feel hurt. Selection of candidates for the ordained ministry can have a similar effect on those who are rejected, for one reason or another. Some men carry a chip on their shoulder for the rest of their lives instead of rolling up their sleeves and sharing in wider ministry with the gifts God has given them and the commitment to him they claim to have. Could it be that the 250 leaders involved in Korah's rebellion were people who had nursed a grievance since the selection of the seventy and the smoldering had now burst out into a conflagration?

Korah attacked Moses and Aaron. "You have gone too far! For all the congregation are holy, every one of them, and the Lord is among them; why then do you exalt yourselves above the assembly of the Lord?" It sounds like very holy talk! It is also remarkably up-to-date. We hear people today argue that there is no need for any form of spiritual leadership or special training or even for church government and that we can all democratically run our own spontaneous groups.

Of course, in one sense that is right. We do believe in the priesthood of all believers. No human priest is necessary to intercede between us and God. Yet we also believe in the Body of Christ and in the many different forms of service within the body for which the Lord gives gifts to the members. Some of those roles are leadership ones, with responsibility in teaching or administration. If we read the New Testament we can hardly think of leadership as unbiblical. True, it is not to be a leadership of "lording it over others" but rather one of humble feet-washing servanthood—but it is still leadership. How can we "manage" the church if we cannot "manage" our own family? Paul asks Timothy. Humility in the body will esteem others better than ourselves and will recognize when God has called some to places of responsibility. This is what Korah would not admit.

How did Moses react this time? Not in complete silence. In any case, Aaron was standing with him. He was not alone. But once again vindication was left to the Lord rather than Moses making his own spirited defense. "In the morning the Lord will show who is his and who is holy and will cause him to come to him."

Moses had no grandiose sense of position. He was not fighting to hold on to his office or role. He was perfectly willing to leave it to the Lord, to go on in the role or yield it, however he willed. It is very necessary for Christian leaders to sit lightly on the "dignity" of their office and to be able to turn to some completely different and humble role in the Lord's service if required.

Nevertheless, having been accused of going too far, Moses returned the compliment: "*You* have gone too far!" The reason for his accusation was that "it is *against the Lord* that you and all your company have gathered." Although prepared to have his role and his conduct put to the test before the Lord, he was also secure in his conviction of the Lord's calling. Thus he saw in this rebellion, a far deeper problem than mere jealousy or antagonism between humans.

For Moses and Aaron the judgment on Korah and the others was an agony of the heart. They fell on their faces to plead with the Lord for his mercy on the people. There was no vengeful spirit in Moses. But no matter how heart-broken he was seeing God's judgment enacted, the people blamed *him* for the loss of lives involved.

Faithfulness in the Lord's calling can be a costly experience. But what emerges clearly from these incidents in Moses' life is that it is possible to keep things in their correct perspective only by keeping our eyes on the Lord, in the constantly-renewed conviction that it is he who has called us. Only that sure, clear-sighted vision given by the Holy Spirit helps us identify the real issues and so promote the glory of the Lord.

Discussion Questions

1. How should Christian leaders react when rivals emerge to challenge their leadership?

2. What are some of the causes of jealousy in a church? How can they be countered?

3. What is the best way to meet human criticism of our leadership?

4. If it seems that criticism of a faith project is more than petty jealousy or pique, but real opposition to God's will, how should it be dealt with?

9
FAITHFUL
IN THE CONVICTION
OF THE
LORD'S VICTORY

Have you heard the story of the two Frenchmen who lived in England for many years? Eventually one of them decided that, since he was going to be in England for life he should apply for British citizenship. His friend teased him about it but went along on the day that the citizenship papers were to be signed. Afterwards he smiled and said to his now-British friend, "Do you feel any different?" The reply: "Well, yesterday Waterloo was a defeat; today, it is a victory!"

When we come into the Kingdom of God we line ourselves up on the victory side. Our God will have the final word. It is his world; he created it and he will wrap it up in his own time. "At the name of Jesus every knee shall bow." Whatever the sufferings and buffetings of the people of God down through the records of history, the Lord will finally vindicate his Word and his truth.

For Moses the conviction of eventual victory and of entrance into the promised land was based entirely on the promise of God. The Lord had said it would happen and that settled it. Deterrents might loom in the form of hunger, hardship, doubt, disobedience and discipline, but nothing could stop the purposes of God from being worked out. There might be delay, but not defeat. It is this fundamental conviction that sustained Moses as the huge and unwieldly nation inched across the desert, step by step.

Now the promised land was within reach and the spies were sent out: one leader from each of the twelve tribes. Their task was to survey the land thoroughly—and to bring back a report of the strength of the inhabitants and their cities, as well as some of their produce (Numbers 13, 14).

The Two and the Ten

After the forty day mission the spies came back and the battle ensued between faith and faithlessness. They all agreed that the land was flowing with milk and honey and their oversized clusters of grapes was produced as evidence. They also agreed in their report that the people and the cities were strong. There was no question about the facts. The question was— how should the people respond to them. Caleb spoke out with clear-cut faith in the Lord: "Let us go up at once, and occupy it; for we are well able to overcome it." But most of the other spies gave the opposite view: "We are not able to go up against the people for they are stronger than we." They exaggerated the difficulties, claiming that the "strong people" were giants who devoured their enemies.

This is a classic example of the "faith battle." It has been repeated many thousands of times in local churches and groups facing some particular challenge for the kingdom. There are those who see the challenge in the darkness of the overwhelming difficulties and those who see it in the full light of the Lord's sufficiency. There is seldom a middle path. In this instance, the difference was this: the ten spies—the majority—saw the difficulties first, and beyond them saw God, but were not convinced the difficulties could be overcome. The two spies—the minority, Caleb and Joshua—saw God first and then saw the difficulties in his light. None of them denied the existence of the problems. They differed over whether God was able to fulfil his promise and give them victory.

That Helpless Feeling

Faithlessness feels so helpless. "*We* are not able." It measures things entirely in human terms. What are our resources? What can we muster in numerical strength? How much money can we raise? Trust is expressed in entirely human and earthly terms.

Faith cannot work on such a basis. It must ask the fundamental question: Is God in this thing or not? Is he leading us or not? Once the conviction of his leading has taken hold of us, there can be no looking back. The unshakeable fact is that if God is in this, he is the Lord who fulfils his promise and leads his people on to victory. Going ahead in faith is not confined to the calculation of our petty resources but is based on the limitless resources of the Lord, who created heaven and earth and who can supply all the needs of his people.

This faith issue has to be fought out in our individual lives as well as in our Christian fellowship. It presses us back to our fundamental belief in God as God. In the faith-project of our buildings at All Souls we found ourselves steadily hemmed in to one and only one possibility. The only way of solving the pressing problem of our lack of space was to excavate beneath the church. The very thought of doing that, in the heart of London's West End, was enough to make one shudder. Indeed, as the plan developed, the estimated cost escalated to what seemed astronomical proportions.

During one of our earlier church council planning meetings God met with us in a very special way. It seemed as if our cold plans and schemes came alight, like a wood fire suddenly bursting into flame. Nearly everyone present on that day knew that the Holy Spirit had come to us, touching us individually and uniting us corporately, so that we were left in no doubt that it was the *Lord* who was leading us into this "impossible" task.

It was that conviction that kept our heads cool, though our hearts were pounding, as we eventually set the architects to work, knowing that the costs would be around three-quarters of a million pounds and we had only £26,000 in hand.

It seemed to some outsiders absolutely crazy, but we knew we had no alternative. The Lord was in this project and we were to follow as he led. We could see the problems only "through" him. If we had calculated according to known human resources we would have given up on the spot.

Such steps of faith are exciting and demanding. There are those who will never associate themselves with such a walk of faith, though they will revel in success when it comes! One elderly church member in Manchester, where God taught us so much about trusting him, said, loudly, dismally and repeatedly: "They'll never do it . . . they'll never do it." But on the day when, by God's grace, the building opened free of debt, he said: "We've done it!"

Faith, on the other hand, lays hold of the fact that the Lord is going to do it even when no human calculation can see *how,* when circumstances seem ranged against the project and when unbelievers pour their scorn or bitterness upon us.

Believing God as God

It is this faith that marks out God's "Honor Roll" in Hebrews 11. Moses is included firmly in the list. So is Noah—how could he have calculated how God would end *his* project? So is Abraham, going out into the unknown, and Joseph, though he is not singled out for being Prime Minister of Egypt but rather for believing that God was going to lead the people out and hence gave directions that his bones be kept ready for the journey!

This chapter in Hebrews starts with the people who embarked on these great exploits of faith; then it tells us of some who received great deliverances by faith—stopping the mouths of lions, quenching raging fire, escaping the edge of the sword. Finally it deals with a third category of faith—one that is often ignored: those who suffered for their faith, were tortured and murdered and left destitute, "of whom the world was not worthy." This is not "success" faith in human terms, but it *is* in divine terms, because the key to all the examples of faith in this chapter is that these people believed in God *as God,* whatever happened. "Without faith," says verse 6, "it is impossible to please God." These people pleased God because they believed him, even in the face of challenge and disaster. They may or may not have known special deliverance or victory in this life, but they all share in the eternal triumph of the Lord and they make up a "great cloud of witnesses" to us, testifying that because they believed God he was glorified through them. They encourage us to run the race set before us, looking to Jesus—there is no other way to keep the faith-perspective.

Back at Kadesh, the "faith" argument went on. The people moaned and complained, foolishly longing to return to Egypt. Joshua and Caleb pleaded further with the people: "If the Lord delights in us he will bring us." They saw once again that the issue was not simply a human one, but was concerned with the Lord and their response to him. Not to go forward would not be simply a matter of prudence but of rebellion against God. The argument is spelled out in unmistakable terms and the faith that "the Lord is with us" is clearly expressed.

The Result of Doubt
What was the outcome? The congregation decided to stone Joshua and Caleb. Faithlessness can be very vicious. One pastor was deeply burdened about some building work that needed to be done in his church. He believed strongly that this was of the Lord but he had some faithless people to deal with in his church and on his church council. At one council

meeting, in desperation at their refusal to go forward, he said, "I believe that if the Lord is in this he will show it to us at once in some tangible and evident form." Next morning a completely unexpected legacy turned up in the mail, sufficient to cover the cost of the project. He joyfully rang up one of his church leaders to tell him. "I told you the Lord would show us," he added. Sourly the answer came back: "You must have known about that legacy last night."

Faithlessness is a miserable business. It misses all the joy, praising and rejoicing, and usually gets more and more sour. Worst of all, as Numbers 14:11 says, it despises God. That is the crunch. The hurt to the pastor could be healed. But *God* was despised. And that brings judgment.

Moses interceded, praying for the Lord's mercy: "The Lord is slow to anger and abounding in steadfast love, forgiving iniquity and transgression. . . ." Pardon was granted but the people would need to understand the deep wrong of what had happened. Instead of entering the promised land they were sentenced to forty years of restless wandering—one year for each of the days the spies spent in the land. And those spies who doubted the Lord would not see the land at all. Joshua and Caleb alone would see the fulfilment of their faith and enter into the joy of the Lord's prepared inheritance.

One wonders how often a Christian project, or the work of a local church, has been harmed or delayed for years because of the faithlessness of its members or leaders. People may look at the church and attribute its emptiness, weakness or powerlessness to the decadent age in whch we live, when quite often the real reason is a failure of faith, a vote of "no confidence" in God, a failure to believe in God *as God,* leading his people and able to overcome any opposition.

"Giants" do not disappear—they have to be tackled. Caleb had the opportunity more than forty years later to prove that his faith in God as an Overcomer was right. In Joshua 14 he asked for his inheritance and even though he was 85 years old he was ready to do what he wanted to do all those years before —go against the Anakim (the giants) and the fortified cities, and show that the Lord is able to overcome. He was still wanting to serve the Lord and his faith was still as strong and true as ever. He still wanted "wholly to follow the Lord."

Often "giants" stand in the way in a venture of faith. They can be official bodies, or people, or other "fortified" circumstances. They need to be tackled in prayer. Each "giant" needs to be particularly and deliberately brought to the Lord. There will often need to be a personal meeting with the "giant," and at such times we will want others to support us in specific prayer. All the "giants" will be reduced to size, and usually will "disappear" altogether. At the very least, their opposition will melt away and the victory will be the Lord's and to his glory.

Ask—and Expect Much More!

God wants people to believe in him. He wants churches to believe in him. Paul gives the ascription in Ephesians 3:20 to "Him who by the power at work within us is able to do far more abundantly than all that we ask or think." That really stretches our vision. Think of all we can expect God to do, ask in those terms—and then expect *much more!* This promise is one of cascading overflow. The "exceeding abundantly" is as strong an expressioin of overflowing as Paul can possibly find. Our God is not a miser who reluctantly doles out a rationed response to our requests, but a God who wants to pour out his blessing and drench us in it, so that we cry out "This is the Lord's doing and it is marvelous in our eyes."

The only limiting factor in this verse is "the power at work within us." It is by the power of the Spirit that we believe in God as God. This glorious promise can never be worked out and demonstrated where there is no faith. But once it is claimed by faith it encourages us to step out into the unknown with him, to see deliverances from bondage, to see the impos-

112 The Moses Principle

sible happen as the waters of our Red Seas part before us, to see the amazing provision and timing of the Lord, to see his planning ahead long before we could have known anything about it, and to see his plans being fulfilled, bringing glory to his name.

Faith in the living God is a great adventure. It is limitless in its possibilities. There are so many areas of life simply waiting for the people of God to enter and triumph in them. The lessons of Moses are lessons for every believer to grasp and apply in his own situation. We are called, as so many before us, to walk by faith in God. It is not a matter of great faith in God—a faith that has to be worked up in some frenzied effort of will. Faith can be as small as a grain of mustard seed. *It is the one in whom that faith is placed that matters.* We are called not to great faith in God but to faith in a great God.

Discussion Questions

1. How should we react to people who see only the difficulties and problems of a faith project? How should we deal with a defeatist attitude in ourselves?

2. What is the essential difference between faith and recklessness? To what extent do normal considerations of common sense and providence apply?

3. How should a church with a faith project deal with opposition from church, government officials or other "outside bodies?"

WARNING!

Ventures of faith are dangerous—indeed, if the Lord is not with us they are disastrous. In Numbers 14:40, the people, seeing they had sinned against the Lord in their faithlessness, decided to act "in faith" and to go up against the enemy in the hill country. It seemed a praiseworthy reaction, demonstrating repentance for their previous unbelief. But one thing was wrong. The sin had been committed and the damage done. They needed to ask afresh whether the Lord was still with them and whether *he* was still leading them to go up to the hill country. Moses told them that in planning to go up now they were *transgressing* the command of the Lord. So they would not succeed. But they presumed to go up. As a result, they brought dishonor on the name of the Lord, for they had to run from their enemies. Any venture which is not within the calling and purpose of the Lord will be disastrous.

It is a salutary lesson. Sometimes people get hold of part of the idea but not the whole. They decide that they will make some matter or project one of faith. Indeed, they may admit that they should have done so in the beginning—and believe sincerely that it will now be completed. "God is God of the Impossible. We believe in him." It all sounds praiseworthy, but there is one thing missing. They have not asked: Is *God* leading? Is this step of faith in his plan? Have they so weighed the circumstances and the challenge and so prayed about it that it seems to them to be *God* who is leaving them no option but to proceed in this way? Then they can step out in faith. But if they do not have that conviction then they can bring only dishonor on the name of the Lord and shame on his people before the eyes of the watching world. Tragically, this has often happened. So let us be warned.

Those of us who have had the privilege of being involved in faith-projects and especially in leadership responsibility within them also need to take warning from Moses himself. It is sad that at the end of his life he slipped momentarily from the God-centeredness that had always marked his leadership, into a self-centered action. "Hear now you rebels, shall *we* bring forth water for you out of this rock?" (Numbers 20:10) It is very easy for us to think *we* have done great things in some sphere of leadership. Personalities are extolled in books and magazines and in the popular mind in the Christian community. As leaders, it is vital that we keep our perspective clear and maintain as low a profile as is possible.

Obviously we cannot avoid being seen and known as leaders but we must never cease to give the glory to the Lord and to express our utter dependence on him. It is sad that this Meribah incident happened and even more sad to hear the Lord's words (Numbers 20:12): "Because you did not believe in me, to sanctify me in the eyes of the people of Israel, therefore you shall not bring this assembly into the land which I have given them." We are all dispensasble, however much we may fool ourselves to the contrary. God's work is far greater than the comings and goings of those he calls to leadership positions; and his glory is far more important than the magnifying or preserving of our personal pride and glory.

PRINCIPLES
OF FAITH VENTURES

1/Sensing the Need

Faith projects are seldom, if ever, luxurious extras. They arise from a real sense of need (as at the Red Sea). The work of God is being obstructed or held up. Often this will be in terms of buildings and facilities, for these are "concrete evidences"—literally—of what God can do. Of course, faith ventures are not confined to buildings.

Is the need as we see it something bearing in upon our hearts from the Lord? Is he calling us to act? Such a conviction may grow over a long period of time or it may arise suddenly in the face of an unexpected barrier to the progress of the people of God.

2/Exploring the Possibilities

We need to look at the situation from every angle—examining every possible idea for tackling it. We may then have to explore these ideas further, translating them into practical thinking. For various reasons we may find obstructions and difficulties until (if this is a venture into which God is calling us) we shall find encouragement from the Lord. Then we shall sense that "the wind of the Spirit is in our favor," and see the first steps of testing the scheme bring positive results.

3/Attaining a Fellowship-understanding
Those who have been directly involved up to this stage now have the task of helping the rest of the fellowship to catch up, to share the vision and come to the same conviction that "this is of the Lord." The way in which the conviction has grown in the leaders needs to be carefully shared with the church or group; the way in which some doors have closed and others have opened needs to be described in detail. In this way, everyone can "walk the same path," seeing how God has brought the group to this point and that they can do nothing but go forward trusting the Lord.

4/Attaining a Fellowship-commitment
Action needs to support words. In the venture of a building-project, for instance, a forward step may possibly be that of "prayerful pledges." These need not be signed. They can simply be made between the individual and the Lord, but offered publicly though anonymously in a pledge-offering service. Some guidelines may be helpful—for example, to think in "units" of $100. The raising of sights needs to be matched by the preaching and teaching of the Word about giving. Once the heart has been set on fire with a project and the Lord's glory has been written on our hearts, pledges are soon doubled and trebled and then left behind in the joy and blessing of giving. Some who feel they can only think in terms of tens end up in terms of hundreds. It is probably no exaggeration to say, "Think of the highest amount you can possibly give—then double it" and you will be nearer what you will acutally give in the end. Other faith-ventures may require a commitment of another kind—perhaps without any money involvement at all—but they are seldom without sacrifice. The

involvement of most members of a church or other Christian group in a faith-venture brings overflowing blessing that will far outweigh any financial sacrifice. God is certainly no man's debtor. It is only those who will not believe or commit who will be sad.

5/A Real Prayer-involvement

No faith-venture can be carried through in our own strength, even though we may be convinced that God is calling us to the venture. The priority of prayer needs to be seen and shared. God's honor is involved as we launch out on a faith-venture. So we shall be deeply concerned to keep to his plan, to see obstacles removed and problems overcome, and the whole venture come to glorious fruition. Then it will be evident to all that only God could have done this thing. We shall organize special times of prayer, perhaps special evenings of prayer once a month, or nights of prayer, or days of prayer, according to the urgency and the local situation. We may encourage the whole church to have a prayer pledge on the same morning each week—wherever they are at the time.

6/Pressing on to the End

Once we have set our hands to the task, the project has begun, and we are involved together, nothing must frighten us. Whatever it is that seems to threaten the progress—whether circumstances, people, opposition from without or within— we must stand firm on the conviction that the Lord has led us into this and the Lord will lead us through, if we remain faithful. We may sometimes wake up in a cold sweat wondering just what we have done in going ahead on this impossible course. Yet as we steady our nerve, laying hold again and again and again of the fact that God has called us into this and that it is not our own idea for which we have sought God's approval, then we have peace in the middle of the storm. As we go forward step by step and see the waters part in front of us we shall know more assuredly every day that the Lord is with us and will bring us through—to his glory.